The
LOW COUNTRIES

THE HORIZON CONCISE HISTORY OF

The
LOW COUNTRIES

96028

by Anthony Bailey

Published by
AMERICAN HERITAGE PUBLISHING CO., INC.
New York

CHAPTER I

AN ACCESSIBLE
REGION

The Low Countries—Belgium, the Netherlands, and Luxembourg —form on a map of Europe a small, unimpressive area, set on the corner of the Continent where the English Channel funnels out into the North Sea. For the most part made up of low-lying land, they have no natural frontiers except the coastline, no exceptional natural features other than rivers, and the rivers are numerous, creating where they meet the sea a sprawling delta, whose islands look from above like the stubby fingers of a farmer's outspread hand. In the northeast the land that is now the Dutch province of Groningen runs with little variation of landscape into northwestern Germany. In the southwest there are no great dissimilarities between country that is now Belgium on one side of a national boundary and France on the other. There is little to make a stranger pause or give him reason to believe that he is entering another country.

This accessibility of the region from land or sea has been important for thousands of years—an advantage for those going there to fight, trade, or settle; a disadvantage at times for those people who were already living in the region. The Low Countries have always been a

The first acknowledged Netherlandish hero, Julius Civilis, accepts his warriors' oath as they prepare to fight the Romans, in this portrait by Rembrandt.

natural crossroads, where people have come together or come into collision with one another. The theme is constant and contrary throughout the centuries of Low Countries history—collaboration and competition; both centripetal and centrifugal forces struggling for preeminence. And perhaps the theme is to be detected in prehistory as well. The distinguished Belgian archaeologist Siegfried Jan de Laet notes that while the unity of the region has always been particularly evident to foreigners, the natives of the Low Countries have never failed to be aware of their own differences.

The first Netherlanders of whom there is some knowledge were by no means as fixed to the spot as later inhabitants. After the last ice age, tundra covered the region, and the nomads who roamed it were reindeer hunters, tattooed users of antler and bone tools, harpooners, occasional dwellers in caves who adorned themselves with necklaces made of perforated wolves' teeth and shells. And as the climate warmed up, and marshes and peat bogs formed behind the new coastal dunes, there were other people—flint workers, and early agriculturalists.

Some settled, for a while at least, in palisaded villages. They made pots and wove crude textiles. Dogs were domesticated. Rudimentary trade began, with stone being imported and flint exported. Their products began to have repetitive, recognizable forms, so that from this distance we can give names to the people of a certain era from the pots that have survived—for example, the Bellbeaker people, who arrived in the Low Countries around 2000 B.C. There were others who made megalithic tombs for their dead, the *hunebedden* of giant stones that are still seen in the sandy countryside of the province of Drenthe. In late neolithic times some villages along the Scheldt River (in what is now eastern Belgium) were settled and remained more or less continuously inhabited into the Christian Middle Ages. Indeed, it seems that in neolithic times the Scheldt region was—judged by sparser standards than today's—quite densely populated. The rivers and the sea were perhaps already having their influence on the local peoples, and so too perhaps was what a later historian has called the "moderate and nerve-steadying" climate.

In the Bronze Age the Low Countries had few raw materials for success—no copper, tin, amber, or gold. But cattle were being bred. In some sections the marshes dried up, to be replaced by heaths and moors. The important trade routes of that era ran elsewhere, but new settlers came, such as the arrivals from England about 1400–1200 B.C. The new-comers brought their own funerary practices to this land of poor farmers. They practiced urn burial; sometimes the ashes of the cremated dead were placed in pots that had been used for cooking. Together with early maritime traditions, one can discern soon enough a tradition of making things go a long way; a habit of having little waste. About 500 B.C. in the Iron Age there were new immigrants from central Europe—Celts and Germans, who settled here and in other sections of northern Europe. Just what the ethnic differences were between these peoples, and where exactly they put down roots, historians cannot say for certain; but it seems that those who about this time invaded the regions of Namur, Hainaut, and Brabant (Belgium's heartland) were warrior folk. In their graves have been found iron swords some three and a half feet long, and horse trappings. Their contemporaries farther north in the Low Countries appear to have been more peaceful people.

The beginnings of historic time depend on written records—on such historians as Tacitus, and Julius Caesar, who wrote his own account of events as he made them. In the early Roman period the Rhine river system formed a rough division between Celtic tribes, or Gauls, living below it, and Germans living above. There are indications of a relatively spartan existence north of the rivers. In the south, an attenuated part of the European Celtic world, people possessed enameled bronze, iron fire tools, helmets, coinage, and heavy, wheeled plows and plow-shares. More Celtic tribes, including those the Romans called the Belgae, had been pushed westward by Germanic pressure in the second century B.C. The Belgae did not in fact pass through present-day Belgium, but Caesar used the name of that tribe to cover all the peoples then living between the Seine and Rhine rivers. He noted that the tribes dwelling along the coast of the Low Countries just then, around 57 B.C., were rough and uncivilized, but courageous fighters. In one battle against the Nervii, one of the Belgic tribes living just south of the Rhine, Caesar and six legions had a hard-fought victory: "Even in their despair the enemy showed such gallantry that when their front line had fallen the next stood upon their bodies to carry on the fight, and when these too were struck down the survivors stood upon the

OVERLEAF: *A lowering sky, a flat, water-laced landscape—ancient features of the Dutch countryside—and windmills, a twelfth-century innovation*

heaped up bodies and discharged their missiles as from a mound or caught and returned our javelins. We must not dismiss as futile the gallantry of men who dared cross a very wide river, climb very steep banks, attack from an unfavorable position: it was their heroism which made such difficult things easy."

Across the Rhine, in the salt meadows of the northern Low Countries, settlers of such tribes as the Frisians were already living on *terpen*, mounds of soil piled up to provide a refuge above sea level. More than a thousand terpen were built between 300 B.C. and A.D. 1100, and on them were constructed farmhouses where the living quarters for men and cattle were under the same roof (as in the farmhouses built in Friesland, in the northern Netherlands, today). These terpen, winter or floodtime places of refuge, became permanent settlements. As the threat of the sea increased, and population rose, the terpen grew larger. One was 20 feet high and 37 acres in area. There are some 180 terp villages and towns in Friesland now, and many smaller terpen with space for three or four farmhouses. The country of the Frisians soon attracted the Romans—Drusus, stepson of the emperor Augustus, led his troops there in 12 B.C. In the layers of the terpen are to be found many pieces of Roman pottery. Trade followed the legions, and no doubt remained after the legions withdrew.

The Romans brought to the Low Countries the advantages of roads, bridges, canals, and dikes, forts to protect them, and villas for the ruling class. They introduced in the southern Low Countries below the Rhine (where the courage of the tribes or the wetness of the north soon caused them to reserve their strength) new methods of cultivation, government, buildings, and commerce. Recent archaeological discoveries in the East Scheldt suggest a flourishing culture. From the estuary bed have been recovered many votive altars to a local goddess with the Romanized German name of Nehalennia. (In the altars, the goddess sits in a highbacked chair, generally with a dog on one side, a basket of fruit on the other. Nautical symbols indicate that she was also a protectress of seafarers.) On the altars are often inscribed the names and occupations of the donors, and so one learns that at that time in the Low Countries there were well-to-do merchants who traded in pottery, fish sauce, wine, and salt. Some had Celtic, some had thoroughly Romanized, names; some were citizens of Trier and Cologne;

one was a shipowner, originally a Gaul from northeastern France who traded with Britain.

While fighting Germanic tribes along the Weser and the Elbe rivers, the Romans settled other Germans on the south bank of the Rhine. To many of these Germans who often served as Roman mercenaries, the Roman Empire was, as the historian Christopher Dawson well put it, less an enemy than a career. Tacitus, the Roman historian, wrote in his *Germania*: "The most conspicuous of all these peoples, the Batavi ... are not insulted by tribute or ground down by the tax gatherer. Free from imposts and special levies, and reserved for battle, they are like weapons and armor, 'only to be used in war.' " The revolt of one such band of the Batavians had little long-term effect on the Roman occupation, but it made a great impression on Tacitus and the elder Pliny, from whom Tacitus got the details for his account. And it made perhaps even more of an impression on later historians. To the eminent seventeenth-century Dutch jurist Hugo Grotius the rising of the Batavians was the first Netherlandish war for freedom. Writing in the nineteenth century, the Bostonian John Lothrop Motley regarded the Batavian revolt as a forerunner of the struggle of the Low Countries against Spanish tyranny. Julius Civilis, the name under which the leader of the Batavians served as a Roman mercenary officer, seemed to Motley a primitive, Netherlandish George Washington. "The spectacle of a brave nation inspired by the soul of one great man and rising against an overwhelming despotism will always speak to the heart, from generation to generation."

But perhaps a keener insight into the actualities of the situation in the Low Countries at the time of Nero's death is to be observed in the fragment of a large painting by Rembrandt. It shows Civilis receiving the oath of allegiance from his men, a hazy red-gold scene of barbaric splendor. (The painting was commissioned for Amsterdam's town hall, but evidently Rembrandt's powerful portrayal of Civilis as a one-eyed guerrilla leader did not fit well with the burgomasters' notion of him as an aristocratic hero, for the painting was soon removed and cut down in size; it is now in Stockholm.) The revolt against the Romans failed, and the Batavian fortress, near the present town of Nijmegen in the southern Netherlands was burned. The fate of Claudius Civilis himself was lost in the lowland mists. For several centuries the Roman peace—with all the ensuing benefits of Roman civilization—lay over the southern Low Countries, where the Gallo-Romans spoke a tongue derived from Latin. Across the language frontier, which has remained to this day, the northern tribes continued to use their Germanic tongues. However, some Latin words were absorbed, and have proved—unlike the Roman roads and bridges in the Low Countries—long-lasting.

Two invasions ended this period. One was the invasion by the sea (which went on rising from the years 300 to 900). It broke through the coastal dunes, widening the delta regions, and causing great loss of land. The other invasion—new waves of Germanic tribes—came after A.D. 250 and overwhelmed (more by infiltration than conquest) the Low Countries. The Angles and Saxons seized the Frisian domains running along the coast as far south as the Scheldt, where the tenacious coastal people had continued to dwell on the sea-threatened land; from this base, parties went on to England. Other new arrivals from the deep forest of Germania, the Franks, pushed westward across the rivers. For

a while they became the allies of Rome, garrisoning, for instance, the Roman fortifications along the Calais-Cologne highway; and becoming, in time, as the Roman authority slowly ebbed, the landowning, ruling class.

The darkness of the Dark Ages following the withdrawal of the last Roman troops, around the year 400, can be blamed largely on the great shortage of written record. The lack of preserved writing presumably reflects the lack of civilization. Perhaps a few hundred thousand people inhabited the Low Countries at this time; a small number of them dwelling on the Frisian terpen; some in the sandy, higher ground to the east maintaining a rough, Germanic peasant life in tribal groups based on villages; and others, in the Romanized western and southern sections of the region, occupying the large country estates. As the Roman centers of administration declined in importance, these estates became a mold, fitting the agrarian tribes into the pattern of landowners and serfs. This shaped much of the western European soci-

Bands of marauding Vikings in river boats clash with one another, perhaps over control of some Low Countries waterway.

ety through the ensuing barbarian invasions and into the Middle Ages.

Christianity was lightly brushed over the Romanized area in the last century or so of imperial rule. After Constantine's decree allowed public worship of Christ, bishops organized several Christian communities along the Lower Rhine and Meuse rivers. But their hold was tenuous. One legend describes how Saint Servatius, the first bishop of Tongeren, was forced to flee from the barbarians to the walled safety of Maastricht, where the saint died and was buried in 384. Although Clovis, king or warlord of the Franks, was converted to Christianity around 493, and baptism after this was considered an act of obedience to the Frankish chiefs, the Christian religion did not for a time spread far or strike deep roots.

Under Clovis and the subsequent rulers of the Merovingian dynasty, Frankish authority extended to include most of what would become France, but the Franks held sway only in the southern corner of the Low Countries. The Frankish kings now and then resided at Maastricht, but their government was not well organized throughout most of the lowlands until the end of the seventh century, when the mayors of the palace—the king's regional administrators—began to assume power. Pepin of Herstal, the Major Domus of the northernmost Merovingian kingdom, eventually prevailed over his rival mayors to reunite the realm. The first of the Carolingian line, Pepin apparently owed some of his influence to large family holdings of land in what Henri Pirenne, the great Belgian historian, calls the semi-Roman, semi-Germanic region around Liège, then a mere village. Several victories over the Frisians also helped establish the authority of Pepin. Charles Martel, his bastard son and heir to the title mayor of the palace, repelled the Arab advance at Poitiers in 732, and found that military success made him master of the Frankish kingdom.

The task of bringing Christianity to the Low Countries took several centuries. Saint Amand, inspired by Irish monks, brought the word to the southern Low Countries, though he was less successful with the fallen diocese of·Tongeren-Maastricht, and gave it up after three years of trying. Many monasteries in this region, Stavelot and Malmédy, for example, were founded under the influence of the abbey at Luxeuil, which with its six hundred monks well deserves Dawson's description as the monastic metropolis of western Europe. At Luxeuil the Irish monk Columbanus founded in 590 a powerful center of missionary activity. From it Irish monks, who were themselves used to clearing forests and cultivating land, went out to convert the peasants—quite likely, as Dawson suggests, by infusing the peasant culture with the spirit of the new religion: "The sacred wells, the sacred trees and the sacred stones retained the devotion of the people, but they were consecrated to new powers, and acquired new associations." Rural Europe was evangelized by these missionaries of the Merovingian age, who often simply provided a Christian ceremony to take the place of a heathen ceremony; underneath it all, the old nature worship kept a long, deep hold.

In the northern Low Countries Anglo-Saxon missionaries had the even tougher task of converting their kinfolk, the Frisians. In A.D. 695 Pope Sergius I gave the bishopric of Utrecht to Willibrord, the Anglo-Saxon missionary from Northumbria in Britain. But when his protector, Pepin of Herstal, died in 714, Radbod, lord of the Frisians, took the opportunity to destroy the churches that Willibrord had founded. (Legend has it that when Radbod heard that, after death, he would not meet his pagan ancestors in the Christian Heaven, he said that he would rather go to Hell and be with his forefathers. The Frisian leader also did not want to submit to the king of the Franks.) Willibrord's successor Boniface was murdered near Dokkum, in Friesland, in 754, in one of the last acts of violent pagan antagonism toward the imposition of Christianity. However, even as late as 896 the bishop of Utrecht was receiving donations to make it possible for him "to instruct and support converts from paganism."

Meanwhile, under Charles Martel, Frankish rule was extended over the coastal kingdom of the Frisians, Angles, and Saxons, and for a brief while the Carolingians dominated the entire, undivided Low Countries. But under this thin skin of political and religious unity that covered their large realm, there remained a good deal of social differences. Probably only in the southern Low Countries were there any estates comparable to the great domains in France where, in these times of constant wars and hunger, the peasants had some protection and an assured share of the soil in return for their hard labor. Perhaps, of the monasteries in the Low Countries, only Egmond, on the northwest coast, in any way matched the great monastic institutions of

France and Germany. In the Carolingian age the monasteries were not only the chief centers of local agrarian economy but also of artistic activity. In them the arts of writing, music, building, painting, calligraphy, and carving were inspired by religious ceremony and given sustenance in an otherwise inhospitable age.

For a little while under Charlemagne and his immediate successors there was peace, though not a very prosperous one. Gold was now scarce. An economy of consumption took the place of an economy of exchange. Commerce became largely regional, based on such markets as that in Aix-la-Chapelle near Charlemagne's palace. However, at the Lower Rhine ports some trade in wine, metalwork, and cloth still went on with Cologne and England. Soft, colored squares of cloth woven by peasants were made into Frisian cloaks, *pallia fresonica,* as they are called in contemporary texts, and were exported from such Low Countries ports as Dorestad, a small fishing village, on the Rhine. Charlemagne, needing a return gift for Calif Harun-al-Rashid, sent a Frisian cloak. The Moslems now dominated the Mediterranean world and long-distance trade was much reduced, but here in the north for half a century from roughly 780 to 834 Dorestad had commercial significance. Although gold *solidus* had been abandoned for the silver *denier,* Dorestad silver coins were popular currency on the Baltic trade routes. For that matter, despite all the contemporary difficulties of commerce, the finest swords found in Viking tombs were those of Frankish manufacture—"the blades of Flanders"—as they were called in Scandinavian sagas.

With the division of the Carolingian Empire among Charlemagne's heirs a line was run through the Low Countries, so that part of them fell into the French and part into the German spheres of influence. But of more dreadful consequence were the assaults of warriors from the north wielding their Flemish blades. The Carolingian conquest of the Frisians and Saxons brought them into immediate contact with the Danes. Tension rose—it was probably aggravated by the land hunger and restlessness that were strongly felt in ninth-century Scandinavia. The Vikings left their homes to coast northern Europe, ascending the navigable sections of the Rhine, Scheldt, and Meuse, among other rivers, and devastating the settlements along their banks. Monasteries were looted; the inhabitants of towns were carried off as slaves. In 808

Guthred of Denmark sent a war fleet to ravage Frisia. The town of Dorestad was pillaged four times in rapid succession in the years 834–837. Then the Rhine changed its course and left the place completely ruined. Utrecht was destroyed and its bishop driven from his diocese. Other natural calamities were reported in contemporary chronicles: "Strange portents were observed in the sky, and were followed by plague, gales and tidal waves. The waters of the Rhine were forced back by the inrush of the sea and drowned masses of people in Utrecht and other places."

After 840 Charlemagne's grandson, Emperor Lothair I, encouraged the Danes to attack the kingdom of his brother Louis, but the Vikings showed little favoritism. The abbeys and towns from Hamburg to Bordeaux were sacked. Great stretches of countryside in France and the Low Countries were laid waste. Things fell apart. In 881 Louis III had a castle built on the Scheldt to bar the Vikings, but he could find no one to defend it. A few years before, a veritable army of Vikings had landed in the delta region and, shifting its base from one fortified camp to another, from Ghent to Courtrai to Elsloo to Louvain, exploited the whole country. Only one small church in southern Limburg survived the devastation of monuments. Lothair II had been unable to repulse the Viking chief Rurik, and had granted him in fief the banks of the Waal River. In 882 Charles the Fat did the same for Godefroid, another barbarian. Although Arnold of Carinthia, the German emperor, finally defeated a late Viking horde at Louvain in 891, and most of the Northmen went on to settle in Normandy and England, they left this part of northern Europe with scorched earth. People drew together, for the population was in decline and there was so much wasted ground. The Roman roads went unrepaired, bridges were down, communications poor. The struggle between Charlemagne's grandsons had been resolved by the Treaty of Verdun, 843, which divided the empire into three equal parts. Much of the Low Countries fell into Lothair's middle kingdom, Lotharingia. But most people were scarcely aware of what kingdom they belonged to; they knew only the local rulers of domain or county. The German chronicler, Thietmar von Merseburg, wrote in those bad times: "This region is justly called the Low Countries, for justice, obedience and love for one's fellowman sink as low as the sun."

CHAPTER II

COUNTS, PRINCIPALITIES, AND TOWNS

Many people in western Europe in the year 1000 expected the world to come to an end. But instead of ending, conditions of life—particularly in the Low Countries—began to improve. To get some idea of what those conditions were, we have to cast out of mind assumptions based on life as it is today. As Marc Bloch, the noted French historian, has pointed out, men of that time were much closer to nature than we are. The rural landscape was rougher, far less cultivated. There were still bears and wolves in much of Europe, and men hunted not just to provide food but to get rid of dangerous animals in their neighborhood. Wild fruit, nuts, and honey were important elements in human food supply. Wood from copses and forests was indispensable for tools and fires. With poor supplies of artificial light, the nights were long and dark. Winters were long and cold. Illness was more serious and more frequently fatal. The poor were poorer and less well nourished; the rich were often overfed. Old age began early; it was a world governed by young men. Natural disasters were frequent, and came with no warning. People commonly (if morbidly) were fascinated by omens, dreams, and hallucinations, but there was little overall

Serfs harvesting wheat for themselves and their overlord on a feudal estate

agreement about a subject as generally important as the measurement of time. The crucial year 1000, when the apocalypse was expected, began in various calendars on half a dozen different dates spread over roughly thirteen months.

There was little social consistency even within areas as small as the Low Countries. The organization of society differed considerably from Namur and Artois in the southwest to Friesland in the north. What Bloch calls feudal society's "vast, hierarchically organized system of peasant subjection and military vassalage" was more in evidence in such parts of the southern Low Countries as Limburg than it was in the northern areas. On the large feudal domains of the southern Low Countries, the peasants were tied to the soil by numerous obligations; but their servitude had its compensations. There was then no state, no government services to look after them, nothing but the earth itself to provide the necessities of life. Under these conditions the feudal domain gave men a measure of protection and assured them some rights to a piece of ground.

In any event, the system of bondage in the Low Countries soon broke down, chiefly because it could not support the growing population— the relative tranquillity that followed the Viking assaults caused a sudden increase in numbers of people and also, presumably, an increase in life expectancy. It was something of a frontier age in the Low Countries. Forests were cleared and the sea pushed back. The first polders were constructed in the county of Flanders about 1150, with dikes being built around the low-lying lands and drainage channels made. In the regions of Zeeland, Holland, and Friesland the same process went on—a communal undertaking, generally, where men worked alongside each other recapturing their drowned land from the sea and making stronger the defense of their farms and villages. In many places the law of the spade was enforced: if you were not willing to help maintain the dikes, you were considered to have forfeited your portion of the land which the dikes defended. The business of reclamation was taken up by the clergy as well; the Cistercian Order began on its formation in 1028 to reclaim and clear the land. And the skill and experience of the Low Countrymen were soon in demand elsewhere. From overcrowded Flanders and from Holland peasants left to drain the marshes along the Elbe River. Counts, bishops, and abbots granted them land and privileges in various parts of northern and central Europe. Flemish colonies sprang up in Pomerania, Saxony, Silesia, and Hungary. The bishop of Bremen and the counts of Holstein and Lübeck summoned the coastal Hollanders to assist them in reclaiming land conquered from the Slavs. In Flanders itself the new land proved highly suitable for raising sheep for their wool. Partly because of the expansive spirit of the age, partly from the reclamations, migrations, and new growth of the towns, serfdom had disappeared from Flanders by the thirteenth century, and feudal taxes were much reduced.

Out of the anarchic maelstrom of the Norse invasions emerged a hardy breed of new leaders—the local counts. As the emperor of Germany and the king of France were proved powerless in the face of the Viking assaults, real authority was assumed by the lords of separate localities. So in the late ninth and the tenth centuries began the age of petty principalities—Brabant, Hainaut, Namur, Liège, Luxembourg, Limburg, Loon, Zeeland, Holland, Utrecht, Gelderland, Overijssel, Drenthe, and Friesland. Sometimes they were friends, sometimes enemies. Once Holland was conquered by the bishops of Utrecht, supported by the dukes of Lorraine, but the count of Flanders helped restore Holland's independence. The counts of Flanders won a reputation for governing their principality with firmness and efficiency; they were also well known for their disloyalty to their feudal lord, the king of France.

One practice of this society was also characteristic of gangsterism in later ages—namely, the "protection" a man received from his lord (often whether he wanted it or not) and for which he paid homage and service in return. Many lords thus had great numbers of henchmen. Flanders, for instance, in this age of chivalry, provided large contingents of roving warriors who were always hungry for a fight. The count of Flanders in 1100 could muster a thousand knights, which was nearly twice as many as the king of France. Flemish adventurers helped the Normans conquer Sicily in 1046, and in 1066 were part of William's army that invaded England—for these services they were granted feudal contracts or fiefs in the form of lands or hard cash. Many Flemish and Brabant knights took part in the Crusades under the leadership of their counts. The Fourth Crusade (1202–1204) was commanded by Count Baldwin IX of Flanders, who was subsequently installed as

emperor of Constantinople (but was killed by the Bulgarians in 1205). From the East, those knights who managed to survive these expeditions against the infidel brought back booty in the form of silver, silks, and spices, a taste for a more luxurious and exotic life, and ideas for such new devices as windmills.

The feudal ties of obligation were intricate. The counts, powerful in their own right, were also vassals. The count of Hainaut, for example, was the vassal of the bishop of Liège, and accepted from his lord gifts of horses, arms, robes, and mantles. It was customary for a knight to entrust one of his sons to his lord—the child was both a hostage and a living demonstration of respect. Thus young Arnold de Guines was brought up in the household of Count Philip of Flanders. As a page, the boy would be instructed in the arts of hunting, war, and courtly manners. Respect and gratitude learned when young made for strong, binding ties.

The ties of kinship were, however, also strong. Marc Bloch suggests that in that violent time, the old barbarian institutions of kin solidarity and blood feuds may well have been revived and provided real cohesion in Flanders, as in northern France. Despite the constant injunctions of the Church, there were numerous family feuds and vendettas. When one noble lady's husband and two children were murdered in Flanders around 1200, the ensuing blood feud shattered the surrounding countryside. Although the saintly Bishop Arnulf of Soissons came to preach reconciliation, the aggrieved widow had the castle drawbridge raised so that she did not have to listen to him, and fighting could continue. Bloch writes, "Among the Frisians, the very corpse cried out for vengeance; it hung withering in the house till the day when, the vengeance accomplished, the kinsmen had at last the right to bury it." Yet even Flemish family blood sometimes ran thin. One knight was turned out of his castle by his two brothers, who murdered his wife and child before his eyes. He managed to kill one of the brothers with his own hands.

Few events of the time had more impact in the Low Countries than the murder of Charles the Good, count of Flanders, on March 2, 1127. The count was cut down by assassins as he knelt in prayer in his church. He was a son of Canute, king of Denmark—which indicates how close relations were in that time along the North Sea coast—and although

This detail from a medieval funeral plaque commemorating an alderman of Ghent conveys a sense of the dignity and pride of the rising merchant class.

he had been invited to become king of Jerusalem in 1123 and two years later to become emperor of Germany, he stayed in Flanders and devoted himself to peaceful government. At Bruges, then a growing town, he lived within the castle walls in a two-story stone house with a church attached. There was a great hall, where he held court, attended by his household officials, and kept his treasure. He attempted to rule with a stern hand the ever-feuding knights, and to suppress their private wars. He forbade them to carry arms in time of peace—which they considered their right. But though his murder seemed the immediate result of a feudal grudge, it, and the violent reaction to it, may have represented the explosive force of the new energies that were just becoming apparent in the Low Countries—in particular, the demands of the burghers of the prospering towns for judicial liberties and economic privileges. On this occasion, the burghers of Bruges revenged themselves on the count's assassins but in the process ransacked the count's property.

The counts of the Low Countries gave their allegiance to the kings of France and the emperors of Germany, and sometimes to the king of England (who was known to pay well). But the giving of allegiance did not always indicate where power lay. King Philip I of France was defeated by Robert the Frisian, count of Flanders, in 1071. Philip, swallowing his pride, was reconciled with Robert and married his stepdaughter. The emperors of Germany often backed the bishops of Utrecht in their attempts to quell unruly local lords. The name "Holland" first comes to light in 1054 as the name of the marshy region over which some Frisian "water-counts" had imposed their rule. From the ambitious Wassenburg family, living between the Maas and the Rijn (as the Meuse and the Rhine are known in the Netherlands), sprang the counts of Valkenburg and the counts of Guelders, while a member of the same family held the episcopal office in Utrecht in the early twelfth century. Soon enough these local potentates came to regard their native lands as hereditary possessions. About this time also, Luxembourg became a countship, and after 1288 it was closely connected with the German Empire.

Only in Friesland were there no hereditary rulers. The Frisians gave their obedience instead to district landowners on more of a terp or village scale. These local leaders had to be confirmed in their position by a meeting of all the householders of the area—a form of democracy. And though both the count of Holland and the bishop of Utrecht saw Friesland as ripe for take-over (and expeditions against the uncouth Frisians were regarded as useful trials of knighthood by young Hollanders), the Frisians resisted these constant invasions. They craftily called for the bishop's help against the count, and made the count their ally when the bishop attacked them. So they remained free.

In the eleventh and twelfth centuries there was a revival of town life and a growth of new mercantile and artisan classes in the Low Countries, particularly in Flanders, a development which quickly gave the region an exceptional character in the Europe of the time. The growth of new cities was encouraged by many feudal princes, who granted charters to places that were potential trading centers—and were thus a possible source of profit to the local lord. The counts often promoted the building of commercial sections outside the walls of their castles. The episcopal cities had been refuges in times of barbarian attack, and there too the *bourgs,* or burgs, that took shelter under the castle ramparts began to flourish—especially where they had not only the advantages of military protection but access to highways and navigable rivers. Bruges gets its name from the *brug,* or bridge, crossing the Zwyn estuary, and traders gathered there, with the added attraction of tax exemptions from the count.

Trade stimulated the nascent industries of these towns, and there were demands for new goods and new ways of doing things. Where merchants congregated, the need existed for butchers, bakers, blacksmiths, and brewers. Urban life made for an inventive, adaptive atmosphere, in which new ideas and processes were encouraged: windmills, horse harnesses (which allowed horses for the first time to pull heavy loads), hinged rudders for ships, clocks, the Gothic arch, window glass. There was a rise in the general standard of living.

At the heart of the increased activity in Flanders was clothmaking, the trade which had been practiced there since the Celtic era. The peasants had preserved Roman processes of cloth manufacture. The Vikings had helped expand the trade in Flemish cloth to the East, which by the end of the eleventh century had reached Novgorod markets. The peasant weavers were the basic work force, though the merchants soon brought them into town.

A rural industry was thus absorbed into the towns, which prospered and expanded. However, as Henri Pirenne noted, the increased population made for increased competition in the labor market; this allowed employers to pay their workers a bare subsistence wage. "The antagonism between capital and labor is thereby revealed to be as old as the middle class." With the rise of an urban proletariat came changes in the old methods of production. The square Frisian cloths were replaced by bolts of cloth forty to seventy yards in length, a more economical size for both making and shipping. (It is reckoned that roughly half the population of Flanders was employed in industry at the end of the thirteenth century, including wives and children who helped spin and weave.)

Obviously this whole new world of trade and urban industry gave the death blow to feudal society. Many men now had ample opportunity to escape agricultural bondage. In Flanders a serf who managed to live in town for a year and a day cast off his servile status. He had a chance indeed for the first time to become a rich merchant or an artisan; one or two had become officials in the count's court. Dependence and poverty were no longer the common man's unavoidable destiny. Yet for many of the workers in the weaving industry, somewhat protected though they might be by their guilds—the associations in which the members of a craft banded together—life remained immensely precarious. There were constant famines, wars, and slumps, interrupting trade and causing desperate unemployment. In 1124, for instance, a horrendous famine struck Flanders. Galbert of Bruges wrote: "Some who tried to make their way to the cities and towns where they could buy bread perished of hunger along the road, choking to death before they were halfway. Near the manors and farms of the rich and the strongholds and castles, the poor—bent low in their misery as they came for alms—fell dead in the act of begging."

After a bad harvest, thousands starved in the Low Countries. Of the year 1196 the chronicler Renier of Liège wrote: "A large number of poor people died of hunger. Animal carcasses were being used as food. . . . No one had hope. A hogshead of rye was sold for 18 sous on June 11th and on the following day for 35. . . . The poor died in the streets. They came groaning in their death agony, lying before the doors of our churches at matins, waiting for the alms that were given

out at the first light of day. This year we have had no wheat since Epiphany." Pirenne calls it an age of constant alimentary crises. Towns and countryside were frequented by beggars, who sometimes roamed in gangs. The name *Brabançons* was applied, often no doubt in a quavering voice, to bands of hungry marauders who descended from the region of Brabant to lay waste nearby provinces of France. There must have been many who would have welcomed in place of their lives of free and brutish vagabondage, the meager, restrictive, but nevertheless protected existence of the feudal estate. Perhaps for want of such an alternative, many Flemings joined the hordes of paupers who made up the shock troops of the early Crusades.

The merchant class was not slow in trying to get rid of the rules and regulations which had been meant for a dependent peasantry and now —as far as they, the burghers, were concerned—simply held back the growth of trade. In Liège and Utrecht and more particularly in the towns of Brabant and Flanders, in Ghent, Bruges, and Ypres, the late eleventh and early twelfth centuries were times of upheaval. Gilbert of Mons says of the burghers of Saint-Trond that they were "right

A French manuscript illustration of 1250 shows knights besieging enemy ramparts as a soldier loads a trebuchet to hurl boulders over the walls.

puissant in arms." (In the face of this puissance, many of the knights, boisterous enough themselves, retired to the country.) The merchants organized guilds, or *hanses,* which were autonomous societies for forwarding their own interests, with powers to collect dues from members. At the guild of Saint-Omer, for example, founded in 1050, members regularly got together to drink and discuss their common interests in their own new *Gildhalle.* In the recently settled commercial burgs and suburbs churches were built to serve the parishioners, with funds supplied by rich merchants. Part of the guild revenues went to pay for town defense works and street maintenance. In Tournai the guild of local merchants took over municipal finances; in other places the burghers began to construct a new machinery for town government. The charters granted by the counts in many towns gave rights to hold courts, and the merchants were able to improve municipal laws. Many odious market tolls, due the counts, were done away with or brought under the control of town magistrates, who were sometimes elected by the burghers from their own ranks, or in some places appointed by the lord. (In Ghent the wealthier burghers soon established an oligarchy, the Thirty-Nine, which governed in three-year shifts of thirteen magistrates. The count of Flanders found them hard to remove.) The old forms of law rapidly changed in the brisk and freer urban air. In the towns the *wergild,* or blood money, was replaced by fines or corporal punishment—which was by no means unbloody: all sorts of tortures and amputations were supposed to deter those who came to town bent on thievery or other knavish behavior.

It was also an age of growing municipal wealth, made proudly evident in the construction of ornate guildhalls and the towers and belfries of the new churches. The men of the Middle Ages expressed their wealth and enthusiasm by founding schools and hospitals; by making a once-and-for-all payment to get rid of tolls and giving princely donations to the great Gothic cathedrals. Money became an instrument of power. The merchants were now in a position to make loans to bishops and counts. The city of Arras in Flanders soon had a reputation for being "avid of lucre and glutted with usurers."

The new schools were mostly for the children of the burghers, but their existence meant that writing and reading were no longer to be skills for the clergy alone; they were needed in commerce too. More-

over, the vernacular language thus came into written use for the first
time, replacing Latin. Although there was this to be said for Latin:
it bridged the language frontier, which had run through the Low
Countries on more or less the same line since Roman times (and on
which it remains till today), dividing the French-speaking people of
Hainaut, Namur, Artois, and part of Flanders from those who spoke
the Low German tongue. Even the latter in the early Middle Ages
could be broken down into many parts: there was Dietsch, or common
Dutch; Flemish, Brabant, and Holland dialects; and further variations
in the eastern regions of Gelderland, Overijssel, and Utrecht. Friesland,
different in this as in many other ways, retained its own Frisian language (which is still spoken there).

The Flemish towns led the development of the Low Countries at
this time. They exported linen, fine wool, cotton, and silk cloth. Bruges,
Ypres, and Ghent were in the forefront, but others gave their names
to their own products: there was cambric from Cambrai, lawn from
Laon, Arras hangings (it is an arras behind which Polonius is stabbed
in *Hamlet*), and Brussels carpet and lace. Soon the native supply of
wool was insufficient, and wool was imported from England. (In
return, Flemish weavers emigrated to England, attracted there by the
clever policy of the English kings.) The English trade connection was
one serious reason why the Flemish merchants and weavers found
themselves in frequent opposition to their count when, from feudal
loyalty, he sided with the king of France against the king of England
in their constant feud.

In Bruges—which in the thirteenth and fourteenth centuries was
the most important commercial town in northern Europe—there were
not only English wool merchants, but Catalans, Venetians, Spaniards,
Florentines, and Bretons. The Hanseatic League, the North Sea and
Baltic trading cartel, had established a post here in 1252; this had between two hundred and five hundred resident merchants, its own
houses, warehouses, and courts. The wealth generated by the cloth
trade created a demand for foreign commodities—fur, tar, timber,
amber, and dried fish from the Baltic; and from sunnier climes, spices,
pepper, cinnamon, ginger, and nutmeg. Although Bruges then had a
good harbor, the native merchants failed to promote their own shipping. This provided an opportunity for other Low Countries towns,

which came into being on natural harbors or well-placed waterways. These settlements were fostered by local lords who like those in Flanders were bright enough to see that increased trade brought increased wealth, some of which unfailingly would accrue to themselves. Thus, without immediately achieving the fame and wealth of Bruges and Ghent, such other towns as Middelburg, Kampen, Zwolle, Zutphen, and Deventer began to prosper from shipping.

Many of the Netherland ports east of Utrecht were members of the Hanseatic League. Moreover, Friesland continued to do well by seafaring. Frisian sailors often voyaged to the Mediterranean, pausing in Portugal to assist the king there with his wars, then going on to the Holy Land. Crusaders often arrived exhausted in Syria to find Frisian ships there with supplies. Adam of Bremen wrote that Frisian seafarers had penetrated the Arctic seas and found lands where the inhabitants lived in caves with great quantities of gold. This gave later Frisian historians the chance to suggest that eleventh-century Frisians had reached Mexico and Peru.

The Low Countries were part of the great medieval Christian world; the Church was powerful and belief widespread. But to some the belief seemed not deeply held, and the crusading spirit insufficient. The fall of Acre in 1291, the last Christian stronghold to be taken by the Saracens, inspired in Flanders a vigorous poem by Jacob van Maerlant, town clerk of Damme, near Bruges. Once Van Maerlant had written chivalric romances; but town life had affected him, and his poem "The Holy Land" was a clarion call to arms, intended to arouse the do-nothing nobility. Van Maerlant wrote (in Adriaan J. Barnouw's vivid translation), condemning the local lords:

> *Forth ye ride, these days, to stalk*
> *The game with falcon and goshawk,*
> *Ye mighty lords and sovereigns.*
> *Hear ye not the Church complain? . . .*
> *Ye lords, this is Jacob's lay, a bit*
> *For you to chew, so bite on it,*
> *Keep this bridle between your teeth.*
> *Let my words sink in, and smart*
> *The cockles of your inmost heart.*

Despise all worldly luxuries.
Too shrill a contradiction it is
To pile up riches and dismiss
The poor and hungry from your mess.

Van Maerlant had a keen eye for the issues of the time. The lords rode out hunting and the ladies of Bruges were, according to the chroniclers, "dressed as queen." There were often occasions for sumptuous pageants or dramatic rituals, as when Count Baldwin accepted the Crusader's cross in the Church of Saint Donation, in Bruges, on Ash Wednesday, 1199, before the assembled chivalry of Flanders. Sometimes holy relics were carried around the ramparts of the town. But despite the fairs and festivals, processions of the clergy, and parades of princes that give rosy color to the age, the poor and hungry were very much there. In 1225, a year of terrible famine, the urban masses thronged to support one Bertrand de Ray, a minstrel who impersonated the hero of the Fourth Crusade, the dead Baldwin IX, count of Flanders, and for several months succeeded in being recognized as a holy prince. Taking advantage of municipal turbulence and Flemish discontent with his daughter Countess Joanna and her overlord, the king of France, the counterfeit count led a crusade through Hainaut, laying waste the countryside and setting fire to churches full of people. Because their daily life on earth was so dreadful, many took comfort in mystical hopes of a millennium to come.

There were urban insurrections on many occasions in the second half of the thirteenth century, notably in Liège, Utrecht, Valenciennes, Tournai, Ypres, and Waesland. The weavers of these towns were often on strike. Yet these people, townsmen and countrymen, had a crude good humor, a keen political sense, and a regard for nature that are to be found in such simple, direct Flemish poetry as "Reynard the Fox," written by the surnameless poet Willem, around 1260. There was a good deal of irreverence, common to laity and clergy. Historian Johan Huizinga notes how one Frisian man of the Church received the news that his concubine had given birth to a son on the very same day that he was elected an abbot. "Today I have twice become a father. God's blessing on it!" said he.

CHAPTER III

FLANDERS
INTO BURGUNDY

Life in the teeming Flemish cities at the beginning of the fourteenth century was full of conflict: between counts and burghers, between burghers and artisans, between the craftsmen of one guild and the craftsmen of another, and between town workers and rural workers. There were conflicts arising from language differences (or masquerading behind those differences), for the upper classes frequently spoke French in the Flemish area, while the lower classes continued to speak the Germanic Flemish. There were conflicts arising from foreign entanglements. The strong trade tie with England was felt passionately by all connected with the wool and cloth industry on which the livelihood of so many depended. The feudal tie with France was generally honored at least in theory by the count of Flanders. Furthermore, among the semi-autonomous towns, or communes, as they were called, there were interurban jealousies; Bruges and Ypres, for example, often found themselves in a serious quarrel with Ghent which, it seemed, had ambitions to dominate Flanders. To make all these problems more acute, the fourteenth century had constant famines, plagues, and the Hundred Years' War between England and France, whose strife often

A bucolic November landscape, rendered by Flemish miniaturists, the Limbourg brothers, for the Très Riches Heures *of the Duc de Berry.*

spilled over into the Low Countries. One may wonder if there was ever a century in which misery was so vivid and so general.

Bells rang daylong in these medieval towns. A bell told shopkeepers to get up before dawn. A bell announced the start and end of the working day. There were some 2,300 weavers in Ghent at the beginning of the fourteenth century, and bells at noon and one o'clock warned everyone to leave the crowded streets so that they were clear for the cloth workers to make their way unimpeded to their homes for the midday meal and back to the workshops. Lateness was a serious offense. With the demand for employment always greater than the supply, it was easy to lose one's job. Bells also announced attacks, riots, and executions. The streets were narrow, the houses close-packed. Although the first bricks were now being exported from Flanders to England, most houses were of timber; because iron nails were expensive, boards were put together with wooden dowels. Many houses could be taken down and put together again; one man in Lille sold his house to another who took it to Ypres. Thatch was banned for town roofs after mid-century, because fires were so common. Markets multiplied; Brussels around 1350 had separate markets for fish, mussels, tripe, chicken, cheese, and milk. Some streets were of cobblestone, and a "Master of the Mud" enforced rudimentary health regulations. Outside the towns the fertile countryside in good years produced wheat, beans, oats, and dairy products. Yet toward the end of the century when problems of trade and urban life had accumulated to such a degree that most of Flanders was depressed, the countryside was affected too. Wild boars ran in neglected fields.

An early manifestation of urban discontent in fourteenth-century Flanders took place on May 18, 1302, and has gone down in history as the Matins of Bruges. Flanders at that time was occupied by French troops, with a garrison in Bruges. Before dawn on the eighteenth, the working people, led by one Pieter de Coninck, a weaver, attacked the French guards, strangled many of the soldiers in their sleep, and proceeded to beat others to death. The French tried to disappear into the crowds but were identified by being forced to exclaim the Flemish oath "*Schild en Vriendt*" (buckler and friend). Many of the town's ruling class—who, although bilingual, perhaps did not have good enough Flemish accents—perished too.

From Bruges the revolt spread. The French king dispatched an army to restore order—an army formed of French knights, the aristocracy of the southern Low Countries, Genoese crossbowmen, and German cavalry. One reason knighthood flowered was because of the introduction of the stirrup, which enabled men in armor to stay in the saddle. But cavalry was not always victorious. On this occasion the Flemish weavers chose their ground well. It was near Courtrai. Canals, marshes, and bogs slowed down the horsemen, and two streams limited the area in which they could organize a charge. The commoners fought in town or parish bands, so that they recognized and supported each other. Their weapons were short pikes or clubs with iron hooks on the end, sardonically nicknamed *goedendags,* good-mornings. These were particularly handy for hauling horsemen out of their saddles. Medieval statistics are not notably reliable, but it is said that the royal army left twenty thousand of their forces dead at Courtrai. The victorious Flemings claimed to have removed seven hundred golden spurs from slain knights; thus the battle has come to be known as the Battle of the Golden Spurs. Its anniversary is still celebrated by Flemish patriots.

In many respects, the century was an almost constant war between the haves and the have-nots, the great and the little. Although the king of France and the local aristocrats soon regained control after Courtrai, revolts and unrest continued. In 1309 a people's crusade got underway in Picardy and the Low Countries, provoked by serious famine and encouraged by the news of a papal expedition to conquer the island of Rhodes as an outpost against the Turks. Armed columns of distressed peasants and artisans pillaged the country. They stormed the castles of noblemen and in many towns killed the Jews, who as money lenders were the natural enemy of the large class of debtors. Further, the Jews, in the eyes of the mob, were still the murderers of Christ. On this occasion, however, the populace met their match in the duke of Brabant, who dispersed the crusaders' army with heavy losses. (A few years before, he had put down an insurrection of cloth workers and buried alive its leaders.) In the 1320s, revolt flared again—this time in the coastal regions. The peasants, both small landowners and tenants, refused to pay tithes. For five years they pursued a dream of rural democracy by driving out the count's officials, burning the houses of the larger landowners, and murdering them and their families.

The prevailing upper-class hatred of the peasantry is evident in a contemporary poem describing the "kermes," or carnival:

> *To the kermes goes the lout.*
> *Then he thinks himself a duke.*
> *And there he lays about*
> *With a rusty stave or crook.*
> *He starts to drink of the wine,*
> *And in his drunken drawl,*
> *He sings, "The world is mine,*
> *City, land, and all."*
> *With bread and cheese, curd and gruel,*
> *They all day stuff their guts.*
> *That makes the churl such a fool:*
> *He never eats but gluts.*

The poem foresees a grisly fate for the Flemish peasants—they will all be drawn and hanged. "Only force can make them behave."

Brave Flemish foot soldiers, some wielding goedendags, *or grapples, fight the flower of French knighthood at the Battle of Courtrai, 1302.*

From the countryside the rising spread again to the towns. At Bruges an insurgent citizenry supported the peasants. In Ypres the artisans drove out the leading burghers and noblemen and set up a government of weavers and fullers—for the moment working together (in 1348 many weavers in Bruges and Ypres were to be massacred by members of the other crafts). The Church was also considered an enemy of the people: abbeys and churches were attacked and burned. One peasant leader, Jacques Piet, said he would never receive the sacrament again; he looked forward to seeing the last priest hanging on the gallows. (This anti-clerical aspect of popular discontent remained a constant theme of the century. Norman Cohn, the historian of revolutionary messianism in medieval Europe, writes, "At Ypres in 1377, cloth workers were not only being hanged as rebels but were being sentenced by the Inquisition and burnt as heretics." For that matter, some priests preached a revolutionary, egalitarian religious message.) Once again the rising was suppressed. The king of France intervened in 1328 after the count of Flanders' counselors had been murdered before the count's eyes. At Mount Cassel (where bloody battles were to be fought six centuries later, in the 1914–1918 war) the rebels were defeated. Although they quickly raised the flag of the lilies of France, the burghers of Bruges had to kneel in the dust for mercy. The town ramparts were broken down; the town charter canceled. Retribution was steady over the next ten years throughout Flanders as the rebels were hanged, beheaded, or broken on the wheel. Nineteen hundred houses were confiscated. Willem de Deken, burgomaster of Bruges, was torn apart by horses on the orders of the French king.

Throughout Europe in these bloody years the common man made many rough-and-ready attempts to improve his lot. The means by which he did so were generally savage and badly organized; the ends were rarely achieved. Although the poor and humble at times gained surprising victories, they hardly ever obtained lasting reforms that would give them a greater voice in affairs of government. (The rise of provincial assemblies in the mid-1300s was more an expression of the growth of the burgher class and the decline of local ruling families. The "communes" were mostly more oligarchic than democratic.)

The confusion and strife that fill this period of Low Countries history were intensified, in Flanders, by the problems of the cloth trade:

OVERLEAF: *The canal- and dike-encircled town of Naarden in South Holland*

unrest at home gave the weavers many inducements to emigrate to Italy and England, where their product would vie with those of Flanders; the Hundred Years' War brought about occasional English blockades, which cut off the supply of wool—the absolutely necessary raw material, without which work stopped; the Flemish towns competed for the wool supplies; and the various crafts fought with each other for pre-eminence, as well as with the merchants for better working conditions and wages. Attempts to organize a fair representation of different groups in the communes or town governments generally fell apart because of mutual distrust between the counts, the aristocrats, the rich merchants, the weavers, and the other craftsmen. They were embittered by class hatred and had little desire to share any power they acquired.

Yet in Flanders one leader appeared who for some eight years led both patricians and weavers. This was Jacob van Artevelde, a wealthy cloth merchant. Assuming the title Captain-General of Ghent in 1336, he formed a government of representatives of the burghers and of the craft guilds. Van Artevelde rallied Flanders behind him, got the English to drop the wool blockade, and declared war on Philip VI of France.

In the face of this, the count of Flanders, Louis de Nevers, fled to Paris. Van Artevelde persuaded Edward III of England to press his claims to the French throne. It was in Ghent, indeed, that Edward assumed the title King of France. His wife gave birth to a son there, John of Gaunt, as the founder of the House of Lancaster was to be called at home. The queen was also godmother to Van Artevelde's son. Van Artevelde's dynamic leadership produced some temporary agreements between Flemish and Brabant towns, emphasizing the need for economic cooperation. Plans were made for a common coinage.

This success and unity, however, were short-lived. Bruges and Ypres were resentful of the hegemony Ghent had assumed in Flanders. Furthermore urban weavers had aroused the hatred of the rural craftsmen and of many urban tradesmen and artisans such as the fullers (who cleansed and thickened the woven cloth by milling it); the weavers insisted on restrictions on the wages and places of work of these other workers. When Edward left for England without repaying a Flemish loan, the men of Ghent turned on their leader. A mob of weavers stormed Van Artevelde's mansion, and, breaking through his guard of Welsh archers, slew him with an axe.

A detail from an altarpiece by Jan van Eyck reveals George van der Peale, portly canon of the Cathedral of Bruges, conducting his spiritual offices.

The story was almost repeated in 1379. This time Jacob van Artevelde's son, Philip, led the weavers of Ghent in an internecine struggle against another count of Flanders, Louis de Maele, and the Flemish craftsmen who supported him. Philip was no simple revolutionary, but lived in the manner of a count. On his country estate he raised peacocks. Music announced him as he went in to dinner, which was served on silver plates. However, these aristocratic overtones of the Ghent rising did not inhibit widespread popular sympathy—a wave of revolution ran from Ghent through Europe. The cry *"Vive Gand!"* was heard in the riotous streets of Paris and Rouen. Despite this support, the Flemish revolt was put down by the French at the battle of Roosebeke in 1382. The white-hooded weavers of Ghent were said to have lost 25,000 men. The French, under Philip the Bold, acknowledged the loss of 43. The figures, at any rate, indicate which side won. For a long time after this, Ghent retained a reputation for being the city of protest. The poet Eustache Deschamps wrote of it:

> *Mad heretic, in all things vain,*
> *Subject to Lucifer's intent . . .*
> *God has willed your sentence plain,*
> *Take heed, false town of Ghent.*

Throughout this period prices rose drastically. The powerful Florentine bankers collapsed in the economic turmoil. Famine and plague struck often—famine had decimated Ghent the year before the battle of Roosebeke. The greatest disaster was the Black Death, an epidemic of bubonic plague, which apparently arrived in Europe from India by way of the Black Sea and the Mediterranean. In the mid-fourteenth century the plague killed between a third and a half of the population of Europe. Corpses lay unburied in the Low Countries as elsewhere, there were so many dead. Out of this catastrophe the only people to profit were the surviving peasants, whose labor was now in great demand. With fewer to farm the land, workers could charge more for their services, though rulers attempted to legislate against this.

The Black Death had a psychological effect as well. Many considered it a punishment imposed by God on a sinful world, and there were frequent outbreaks of religious fanaticism. Processions of flagellants preceded the plague in many places in Europe, passing in waves of emotional agitation from town to town; the agitation often multiplied in intensity as it moved on. It was a masochistic form of mass penitence. The flagellants beat themselves rhythmically with leather scourges to which iron spikes were attached. The ceremonies of flagellation were solemn rites, accompanied by hymns. People regarded the flagellants as martyrs, taking on the sins of the world, and they approved of the bloody, self-inflicted wounds. Fifty-three hundred flagellants arrived in Tournai in one two-and-a-half month period, and one Low Countries monastery fed 2,500 flagellants in six months.

This fanaticism had dangerous side effects. There were frequent attacks on the clergy and church property, and on Jewish communities in many European cities, particularly Mainz and Cologne. In Brussels the approach of a wave of flagellants, together with a rumor of well-poisoning, launched a violent assault on the town's Jewish community. Despite the efforts of the duke of Brabant to quell the violence, six hundred Jews were killed. Flagellant processions and ceremonies in many sections of the Low Countries turned into massacres in which as many Jews as could be found were burned or drowned. Norman Cohn reckons that after the panic of these years very few Jews were left in Germany or the Low Countries.

As the grim fourteenth century drew to a close, there were, however, a few cheerful prospects. Wars between one region and another, or one class and another, did not interfere with growing cooperation in the war against the elements. For instance, drainage and flood protection works were made in collaboration by Holland and Utrecht. The prosperity of the coast region was pushed forward by Willem Beukels of Zeeland who is said to have invented the salted herring which could be stored for a long time and safely shipped great distances.

In this period the Low Countries were still immensely influenced by France and Germany, whose rulers remained the overlords of the lowland principalities, though in return those principalities did occasionally provide the emperor. Several counts of Luxembourg were elected to that post. But now too the Low Countries began to exhibit signs of national differences. Of course, few men from the Low Countries would claim citizenship of anything larger than the town in which they lived. But some of the international aspects of the Middle Ages began to wane. In 1270 the Bible was translated into the Flemish vernacular. Moreover, although Gothic architecture in the Low Countries showed strong French or Rhineland influence, the immediate locality had its own effect. In most places "Gothic" had to be adapted to Low Countries requirements; since stone was lacking, and the marshy soil was less suited to heavy structure, the region's buildings were simpler, built of brick rather than stone, less Gothic in their lowness and broadness, and with timber roofs instead of stone-ribbed vaulting.

There was now also visible the work of Low Countries artists. Jean Bambol, born in Bruges before 1350, heralds a Franco-Flemish school of painters. Masters from Brabant, Hainaut, and Limburg were attracted to the French court, which offered patronage. A high point in what survives of the art of that time are the miniature illustrations of the *Très Riches Heures du Duc de Berry.* Here, in the tiny masterpieces which the Limbourg brothers, Pol, Herman, and Jehanequin, executed around 1415, for the brother of Duke Philip of Burgundy, begins the tradition of exact and loving observation that following generations of Flemish and Netherlandish painters have honored and sustained.

In the century after 1385 the French dukes of Burgundy with much accompanying drama brought the towns, provinces, and principalities of the Low Countries under one rule. Through four generations the Burgundian dukes acquired—by marriage, alliance, inheritance, and conquest—a goodly part of what in Carolingian times had been the Middle Kingdom, Lotharingia. Philip the Good, the third duke to rule, wanted to create a second France between the Alps and the North Sea —a country that would rival France and provide the basis for its ruler to have at least equal glory to the king of France. Having already got his grip on Flanders through inheritance, Duke Philip forced Countess Jacoba of Holland, Hainaut, and Zeeland to recognize him as her heir; with that arranged, in 1433 he demanded (and received) her abdication. He had obtained Brabant in 1430 when the duke of Brabant died without issue. He purchased Luxembourg in 1445. In 1456 he had his bastard son David appointed bishop of Utrecht. His son and heir, Duke Charles the Bold, seized Gelderland and Lorraine.

So, through the work of this vigorous family, the ramshackle political arrangements of the early Middle Ages began to give way to something more unified and compact, with a strong central government

Bruges, which translates as "bridge," and was once a major port on the Zwyn estuary, still retains the appearance of a medieval town.

increasingly run from Brussels. Through their court and administration, the Burgundian dukes fostered the spread of French civilization; but they tried to make their realm independent of France and Germany, and they encouraged a great deal of native talent in government and the arts. They established a high court of justice; they attempted to create a uniform currency throughout the Low Countries; and they founded in 1425 the first institution of higher learning in the Low Countries, the University of Louvain.

Although, in the preceding hundred years, small provincial assemblies, or States, of nobility, clergy, and burghers had met to discuss their common interests, Philip the Good convoked a States General to deal with a tax that would be levied on all his territories; he did this instead of convoking a separate assembly for each province concerned. The dukes also subordinated the provincial financial comptrollers to a Central Chamber of Accounts set up (like the new high court) in Malines, midway between Antwerp and Brussels. The States General were asked on several occasions to supply funds for the maintenance of a standing, mercenary army, and on two occasions out of three they agreed, albeit reluctantly, with the dukes' demand. It was a concession to the unifying principle. However, when Philip the Good imposed a salt tax, to replace an annual grant voted by the States, there was much opposition. Ever-rebellious Ghent fought the duke over the matter, but surrendered when his troops took the city. Two thousand citizens of Ghent were forced to kneel in their shirts before the duke. He imposed a heavy fine and took away from Ghent its right to control the surrounding countryside.

The new state created by Burgundian persistence depended on new men—on a new provincial aristocracy which the dukes fostered, raising up, among others, the Nassaus of Breda, the Egmonts of Holland, and the Ravensteins of Guelders. The provincial councils that assisted the stadholders (the dukes' representatives) were made up of noblemen and burgher lawyers. The latter in time became—through their knowledge of jurisprudence and administration—the core of the ducal government. Curiously, the realities of feudalism were fast disappearing from the government of the Low Countries while the outward forms of feudalism were not only being preserved but made much of.

This was so much the case that many took the outward manifestation

for the real thing. Georges Chastellain, a chronicler at the court of the
Burgundian dukes, gives the impression that the Burgundian fortunes
are based on heroism and devotion to knighthood—with no acknowl-
edgment of the skillful administration or the wealth of the Flemish
and Brabant towns. The flamboyant pageantry acted as camouflage for
the real moving forces of the time. The names the courtiers pinned on
the dukes—the Bold, the Good, the Fearless, and so forth—were, as
Huizinga pointed out, "Inventions calculated to place the prince in a
nimbus of chivalrous romance." Charles the Bold, the last of the dukes,
sat in audience two or three times a week archaically administering
personal justice. In his youth, he had had his attendants read out to
him the exploits of Sir Gawain and Sir Lancelot; and though, later on,
he came to prefer the ancient authors, he continued to take seriously
the emulation of chivalry. Philippe de Commines, another chronicler,
wrote of Charles the Bold: "He desired great glory, which more than
anything else led him to undertake his wars."

The ducal desire for prestige was well served by their love of pomp

*Workers portrayed in a late-fifteenth-century Flemish miniature stir their
fabrics in a vat of hot dye.*

and display. The Order of the Golden Fleece, an aristocratic club with limited membership, was founded by Duke Philip to symbolize his power—and also to rival Louis, duke of Orléans', Order of the Porcupine and the duke of Bourbon's Order of the Golden Shield. The exclusive rites of the Golden Fleece were highly religious. The knights sat in choir stalls at masses and obsequies. They wore vermillion robes lined with gray fur. The fleece itself, hung from a chain around the neck, symbolized (in the rather abstract, dreamlike way of the later Middle Ages) the Lamb of God, the Old Testament fleece that Gideon spread to receive the dew of Heaven, and the fleece that Jason and the Argonauts went seeking. And perhaps it had a firm basis in the wool that went into the cloth of Flanders.

Spectacular pageants were often held, as on the occasion when Philip the Good married Isabella of Portugal in 1430. Moreover, at Philip's court ceremony was all-important and ornate. He was served on bended knee. Every object presented, whether letter, towel, or cloak, had to be kissed by a series of gentlemen in waiting. But he had, despite the display of prodigious banquets, a modest appetite; it was observed that though he rose at 6 A.M., he sometimes ate nothing until 4 P.M. He also had eighteen of his illegitimate children raised in the court.

Tournaments and processions, festivals and masquerades, were highly popular. When Philip and his bride Isabella came to Ghent, after his victory over its people at the battle of Gavere, they made a triumphal entry into the pardoned city. Minstrels and musicians lined the walls and the clergy sang a *Te Deum* at the gate. Along the route of the procession through the town stood platforms on which actors performed various historical and biblical dramas, among them the parables of the prodigal son and Caesar among his senators. On a three-story platform in the market place, curtains parted as the duke and duchess went by, revealing a *tableau vivant* of the masterpiece Jan van Eyck had recently painted, "The Adoration of the Lamb."

The various craft guilds and corporations competed with one another at these shows. Many of the burghers belonged to Chambers of Rhetoric, which were local poetry and drama groups whose dining and drinking accompanied artistic jousts. The state wedding reception held at Bruges for Charles the Bold and Margaret of York was like a Disneyland production. One attraction was a huge banqueting house carried by barge from Brussels and decorated by artists from Flanders, Artois, Brabant, and Hainaut. There was a forty-foot-high tower crammed with mechanical monkeys, wolves, and boars, which danced and sang.

"All aristocratic life in the later Middle Ages is a wholesale attempt to act the vision of a dream," says Huizinga. But the attempt could not always disguise the down-to-earth aspect of things. Charles VI, after the bloody battle of Roosebeke, asked to see the corpse of Philip van Artevelde. He kicked the body, "treating it as a villein," one chronicler writes; later the corpse was removed from the field and hung from a tree. With immense relish the nobility watched a judicial combat between two burghers; one savaged the other, and the dying man was taken from the arena and hanged.

The knights of this time went into battle hoping to capture noble prisoners who would fetch high ransom prices. It was perfectly possible to treat life as a fairy story, as Charles the Bold seemed to, and then, in the proud pursuit of military glory, raze Dinant to the ground and have its inhabitants tied together in pairs and thrown in the Meuse to drown, as Charles also did. In 1468 at Liège he sacked and burned the entire city, slaughtering and drowning its people. In Ghent, a year later, he had the leaders of the town on their knees, trembling for their lives, as he tore up the town charters. But he was not unlike his people. Townsfolk and peasants thronged to tortures and executions. The people of Mons paid good money for a brigand so they could enjoy seeing him quartered. At Bruges in 1488 citizens had an excellent time watching their magistrates, who were suspected of treason, being tortured on a platform in the market place. The magistrates begged to be put to death swiftly, but this was refused them.

In that time there were no qualifications or doubts about criminal responsibility; no mitigation, only the extremes of mercy and the cruelest punishment. It was a reflection of a world of stark contrasts. Consider the Flemish illustration (c. 1500) to the "Roman de la Rose" which shows Venus being pulled in a wagon by a team of doves—love assisted by peace—while in the foreground soldiers march, and in the stormy sky behind, vultures wheel, presumably over a field of dead. Life smelled of blood and roses.

For the people of that period life, like the afterlife, was either Heaven or Hell—all or nothing, one way or another. During the papal

schism, the town of Bruges officially went over to the obedience of Avignon. Although no dogmatic problems were involved, many disaffected Bruges citizens left their houses and their jobs and went to live in one of the towns supporting the camp of Pope Urban VI.

The violent, no-compromise policy of the dukes of Burgundy reached a peak in the reign of Charles the Bold. "He was very splendid and pompous in this dress, and in everything else, and, indeed, a little too much," wrote Commines. "He paid great honors to all ambassadors and foreigners, and entertained them nobly. His ambitious desire of glory was insatiable, and it was that which more than any other motive induced him to engage eternally in wars. He earnestly desired to imitate the old kings and heroes of antiquity, who are still so much talked of in the world, and his courage was equal to that of any prince of his time." Charles the Bold's courage, boldness, or foolhardiness brought him to his death on the battlefield of Nancy, fighting the Swiss in 1477. The constant wars, massacres, misery, and disease gave rise to a general feeling of calamity and doom. Even at court this was felt. Chastellain writes in the prologue to his chronicle: "I, man of sadness, born in an eclipse of darkness. . . ."

And yet "Burgundian civilization" is not too grandiose a term to apply to the Low Countries in this period. The dukes were great patrons of the arts, which flourished in that intense and passionate urban atmosphere. The artists belonged naturally in a world of artisans and craftsmen—weavers, potters, dyers, metalworkers, blacksmiths, boat builders, and masons. Men came from various parts of Europe to be apprentices in the Low Countries. Albrecht Dürer's father served his apprenticeship in a Netherlands' goldsmith's shop before settling in Nuremberg. Skills were inherited, improved, and passed on. Jan van Eyck, for example, came from the vicinity of Maastricht, where the skills of illuminating manuscripts had long been practiced. Van Eyck served the dukes of Burgundy not only as a court artist but as a diplomat. In his work, oil paints were used, perhaps for the first time, to convey the most intimate truths about the appearance of water, silk, tiles, and human skin. In the backgrounds of his paintings there is often a landscape. Beyond the two seated figures in the Louvre painting by Van Eyck known as "The Virgin of Chancellor Rolin," one looks out through a colonnade, over a balcony, at the river passing

"The Legend of Saint Eligius and Saint Godeberta," portrayed by Petrus Christus in 1449, reflects the opulence of a contemporary Antwerp jewelry shop.

under bridges and between gardens into the misty distance. Suddenly nature—or man's ordering of nature—seems to have been discovered as something aesthetically pleasing. There is also a small windowful of landscape in Hans Memling's "Virgin with an Apple," now at the Sint-Jans-Hospitaal, in Bruges. The interiors shown in these paintings provide numerous interesting details. From Rogier van der Weyden's "Annunciation" and Van Eyck's double portrait of Giovanni Arnolfini and his wife, one learns about the tiles on the floor, the carpentry of settees and beds and sideboards, the molding of mantlepieces. Yet there is still something here that is not "modern"—a feeling of no oxygen in the air; a stillness; sensations of an enclosed world where things went round and round but not forward. The idea of progress had not, it seems, been taken up as yet.

Wealthy bourgeois patrons and buyers emulated the dukes, and the artists were drawn to the magnet of Flemish prosperity. Memling came from the Rhenish city of Mainz to live in Bruges, Gerard David came from Oudewater in South Holland to Bruges, and Dirk Bouts from North Holland's Haarlem to Louvain. Orders for altarpieces and portraits were placed by churches all over Europe and even from the distant Canary Islands. Many European merchants and bankers commissioned portraits of themselves and their wives: in one painting, as in Van Eyck's "Betrothal of the Arnolfini," or separately, as in Memling's superb twin portraits of the Portinari, now in the Metropolitan Museum, New York.

Architects and sculptors were also given many opportunities to express their talents. Among the outstanding craftsmen, who produced such works as the carved corbels of prophets on the new Brussels Town Hall, was young Claes Sluter from Haarlem. He trained with the Brussels guild of stonecutters in the late 1370s and went on to become court sculptor to Philip the Bold at his Dijon seat. Among Sluter's masterworks is the Column of Prophets, (also known as the Moses Well), at the Carthusian monastery of Champol, near Dijon. In this period town halls and churches dominated the plains of the Low Countries, with spires and belfries. Cathedrals, noble halls, and merchants' houses were hung with tapestries from Brussels and Tournai.

At Brussels Philip the Good founded the Burgundian Library, which still graces the city. He gave pensions to artists and brought musicians

In an age that still attested to the efficacy of the magic arts, an anonymous artist depicts a comely maiden preparing a love philter.

to his court, including such notable contemporary composers as Jacob Obrecht and Johannes Okeghem, whose music found its inspiration in folk songs. The words of the popular songs were in the Flemish Dutch vernacular—what the snobbish courtier Chastellain called "peasants' talk," as spoken by the "people of the pastures, the ignorants, rough of mouth and palate, of poor appearance, as suits the nature of the land." But in fact this period marks a high-water mark in Low Countries' bilingualism. The dukes, although of French blood, encouraged the use of Flemish in order to stress their independence of France. At the jousts organized between the Chambers of Rhetoric of rival towns, both French and Flemish would be in use.

On one side the Burgundian renaissance presents a picture of a new kind of life, rich and prolific—a time of indulgence in luxury, social festivities, elegance in clothes, and comfort in houses, and a widespread relaxation in morals. Duke John II of Cleves had sixty-three acknowledged bastards. The upper-class men wore padded doublets and tight-fitting hose (Philip the Good was also nicknamed "Long-legged Philip"); the ladies had enormous headdresses and low bodices. Yet also prevalent was a belief in witchcraft and black magic, and, particularly among the merchants and the common people, an authentic religious spirit. The Nuremberg doctor Hieronymus Munzer, who visited Bruges at the end of the fifteenth century, wrote: "They are much given to love and also to religion, for in these regions of the northwest, people are wont to go to extremes—all or nothing."

It was in the Low Countries that a medieval heresy called the Free Spirit flourished longer than elsewhere. It was a form of mystical anarchism; believers came to think that they had attained such perfection that they were incapable of sin. In Antwerp around 1230, for example, one Willem Cornelis declared that monks who did not observe perfect poverty were damned to hell-fire. However, anyone who did lead a life of absolute poverty could sin as much as he or she liked. Cornelis himself was said to have been "wholly given up to lust." By this principle the rich were infallibly damned; the poor were in a state of grace that no crime or carnal indulgence could impair. Perhaps it made up for some of their poverty.

Such heresies now and then helped stimulate forms of religious activity. The cult in Brabant that surrounded the Free Spirit adept

Bloemaerdinne brought eloquent opposition from the great fourteenth-
century mystic Jan Ruysbroeck. Ruysbroeck, who lived near Brussels, in turn was the teacher of Gerhard Groot. Groot founded a religious movement called the Devotio Moderna, one of whose aims was to give people—who might otherwise have been involved in the heretical Free Spirit movement—an orthodox way of fulfilling their religious needs. In the IJssel River towns of the northern Netherlands adherents of this movement organized themselves as the Brethren of the Common Life and became a powerful cultural force in the Low Countries during the fifteenth century. Forerunners of the Reformation, they pursued the ideal of a simple religious life, opposed not only to heresies such as the Free Spirit but to the wealthy, politically connected ecclesiastical empires of the Burgundian bishops. Groot and his disciples formed a community at Deventer. This was copied by other fraternities elsewhere in the Netherlands. Among other things, it inspired the spread of education and literacy. The Brethren set up boarding schools which helped propagate humanist ideas among the growing middle classes.

The Brethren of the Common Life are also credited with helping bring about a monastic revival, and with inspiring the compilation of devotional and mystical experience put together by the monk Thomas à Kempis—*The Imitation of Christ*. And the Brethren's work is paralleled in the labors of many itinerant preachers who traveled through the Low Countries in the second half of the fifteenth century, denouncing the morals of the time and the behavior of those in high places, both lay and religious. One such preacher, Jacob Brugman, belonged to the reform wing of the Franciscan Order, which wanted to make the friars take seriously the standards set by Saint Francis. Brugman preached to all who would listen on the virtues of a simple, good life, and his preaching clearly had an effect. "To talk like Brugman" is still in this century a proverbial Dutch way to express admiration for a person's eloquence. Furthermore, Jacob Brugman and Gerhard Groot draw our attention to the birth of an element that will come to seem particularly notable in the Low Countries. This is a tradition of brotherhood and tolerance, of moderation and humanity. It is a sign of things to come when Thomas à Kempis writes, "Whoever loves much, does much. Whoever does a thing well, does much. And he does well, who serves the community before his own interests."

MAXIMILIANVS I IMP.
ARCHIDVX AVSTRIÆ
DVX BVRGVNDIÆ.

PHILIPPVS HISP. REX. 1.
ARCHIDVX AVSTRIÆ.

MARIA D
BVRGVN

FERDINANDVS I. IMP.
ARCHIDVX AVSTRIÆ

CAROLVS V. IMP.
ARCHIDVX AVSTRIÆ.

CHAPTER IV

THE HAPSBURG
SLEIGH RIDE

The battle of Nancy, 1477, marks the end of Charles the Bold's attempt to make permanent the link between the Low Countries and the home of the dynasts, the duchy of Burgundy. The heir to the martial last duke was his daughter, Mary of Burgundy. But the States General, with little gallantry and resenting the high cost of her father's ambitions, took the opportunity to make Mary sign a document called the Great Privilege, which ensured their ancient rights, customs, and liberties—or so they hoped. The States General also decided to counteract growing French pressure by insisting that Mary marry Maximilian of Austria, the Hapsburg prince who in 1493 was elected emperor. Thus began what one historian has aptly called a genealogical joyride; though for the Low Countries themselves there was not always much joy in the process. The succession went in this manner:

Mary *(married Maximilian of Austria)*, 1477–1482
Philip *(son of Maximilian)*, 1482–1506
Margaret *(daughter of Maximilian)*, regent, 1506–1530
Charles V *(son of Philip)*, 1519–1556
Philip II *(son of Charles V)*, 1556–1598

Three generations of Hapsburgs in this portrait include Maximilian and Mary, above, flanking their son Philip, and his son Charles V, below center.

What might happen to a small country once its destiny was mixed up with European royal families is indicated in the case of the Low Countries under Philip I and Joanna. From his mother, Philip inherited the Burgundian possessions. But a few years after Philip's marriage, his wife Joanna, daughter of Isabella and Ferdinand, inherited not only Castile but Aragon, Sicily, Naples, America, and the Indies. So when Charles V came of age, he inherited from his father, his mother, and his grandparents a great empire. He was, at once, prince of the Netherlands, king of a united Spain, and emperor of Germany. The Low Countries were merely a small, if wealthy, section of his vast domains, but they were involved willy-nilly in the long Hapsburg quarrel with France. Perhaps if the States had foreseen the results of what—for some of the provinces—would be the three-centuries-long Hapsburg connection, they would never have pressed Mary into her marriage with Maximilian. Rubbing in that aboriginal mistake, Louis XV of France declared as he stood at Mary's tomb in Bruges, "There lies the cradle of our wars."

For a while after the debacle at Nancy it seemed that the Low Countries were going to retreat into their medieval parochialism. The Flemish towns reasserted themselves. Louis IX of France decided the time was ripe to win new possessions. The Burgundian unity crumbled. After Mary's death (following a fall from a horse) in 1482, Maximilian had to struggle to remain regent of the Netherlands—his real claim to continued authority resided in the fact that he was the father of Mary's children. His son Philip was forced to do homage to King Louis XI of France, and his daughter Margaret was betrothed to the dauphin. But when the Flemish towns rebelled, and Bruges took Maximilian captive, help came from his Hapsburg family. The German states sent troops to punish this assault on their emperor-to-be. And though they restored Maximilian, their presence also began to provoke common resistance.

In both direct and indirect ways, Hapsburg policy did much to draw the Low Countries together. Charles V continued the tradition of the dukes of Burgundy and his grandfather Maximilian in showing little respect for the ambitions of the towns and provinces to maintain their own rights and semiautonomous governments. Although he continued to summon the States General (which remained—in his frequent absences—a potent political voice), Charles neglected few occasions for squashing dissent against his centralizing policy—as for instance in 1540 when he punished the town of Ghent. Charles had applied to the States General for a subsidy to finance his wars. All the members agreed, but Ghent spoiled the unanimity of the Flemish delegation's vote by refusing; the town rebelled. Charles sent his troops and had nine of the ringleaders executed. Ghent forfeited its constitution, ancient liberties, and rights over the surrounding countryside, as it had done under Philip the Good. It paid its share of the subsidy. Charles also gathered in new possessions. He took over the dissident Frisians, the territory of the bishop of Utrecht, the province of Groningen, and the widespread lands of the duke of Gelderland, Charles of Egmont. This nobleman had the aid of the French king and many Low German princes, and gave Charles a long, hard fight. The eastern frontier, which has since prevailed with Germany, was thus defined. Charles also got King Francis of France to renounce his feudal suzerainty over Flanders and the other fiefs, which had traditionally owed loyalty to the French Crown.

The centralizing tendency was also to be seen in the Hapsburg administration, which provided many jobs for the career-minded. There was a Council of State, whose members were all nobles of the highest rank, and which was consulted by the monarch or his regent on matters of general policy. There was also a Privy Council, staffed by lawyers which met daily and formed the chief administrative organ. A shake-up of the ecclesiastical system withdrew Low Countries dioceses from the authority of German and French archbishops and gave the archbishoprics to native princes of the Church. In 1548 the emperor formalized the unity of the Low Countries by having the Diet of the empire approve a decree making the provinces a separate *Kreis,* or "Circle," of the empire. A few years later the States General of all the provinces approved another decree which made the same rules of succession apply in each province, and thus ensured that the Low Countries would not be partitioned as a result of the emperor's death. In this way the state of the Seventeen Provinces of the Netherlands came into being (though no historian seems to agree with any other as to what, exactly, those seventeen are; some now claim that "seventeen" is simply a figurative way of saying many, as in Seven Seas.)

In other ways Hapsburg policies proved divisive; the imperial rule produced local antagonisms. The sense of being subjected to a foreign, mostly absentee, ruler inspired the development of patriotic sentiments. As in North America under British rule, the concern for money went along with the desire for independence. In 1534 the province of Holland, through its representatives, rejected Charles' proposals for greater unity because (they declared) "in case of a war with France, all the taxes levied on Holland would go to the other provinces." The States Assembly of Holland claimed that they would rather be involved in a smaller alliance with Brabant, Friesland, Overijssel, and Utrecht. It was an early sign of a distinct grouping of the northern provinces. The distinction was accentuated by the fact that Brussels, in the south, was the favored capital of the Hapsburgs and the regents who looked after the Low Countries during their prolonged absences. And though Charles had regional representatives, the stadholders, in the northern

Dutch interests in world exploration are reflected in this still life.

provinces, these officials were invariably picked from the ranks of the southern nobility, who were French in speech and culture.

Although they did not spend a lot of time in the Low Countries, the Hapsburgs found them more valuable than any of their other possessions in the increasingly difficult business of financing their foreign wars. Between 1520 and 1530 the Low Countries provided Charles V with fifteen million *livres tournois*. Annually they contributed to the royal exchequer roughly four times as much as the combined revenue from the Indies and Spain. This did not include the loans they also raised. Indeed, the bankers and merchants of the Netherlands, particularly those of Antwerp, were more profitable than the gold mines of Mexico and Peru.

This was the age of Antwerp. "Every period and society has some particular center, or institution, or social class, in which the characteristic qualities of its genius seem to be fixed and embodied," R. H. Tawney, the economic historian, has written. "In the Europe of the Reformation it was the Low Countries. The economic capital of the new civilization was Antwerp." A Venetian envoy remarked, "I was astonished and wondered much when I beheld Antwerp, for I saw Venice outdone." C. V. Wedgwood writes, "For nearly a century . . . this cosmopolitan city controlled exclusively the money market of the known world, and the whole varied interchange of goods and wealth. Every nation had concessions within the walls, every important loan in Europe was negotiated here."

The other cities of Flanders had suffered a great deal from English cloth competition, and from the rivalry of rural looms. Bruges was particularly troubled because of the silting of the Zwyn estuary. But during the civil wars after the death of Charles the Bold, Antwerp— on the navigable Scheldt—stayed to a large extent loyal to Mary and Maximilian. In 1488 Maximilian rewarded the city with a charter which ordained the transfer from Bruges to Antwerp of all the trade of the Netherlands. The charter invited the foreign merchants residing at Bruges to move to Antwerp, where they were assured of the same privileges they had enjoyed in Bruges.

In fact, there were far fewer restrictions and much greater privileges in Antwerp. The medieval ordinances of Bruges and Ghent were here replaced by free trade. England was the chief partner, providing not

only cloth and wool but tin, lead, sheepskin, rabbit skins, all kinds of fur, leather, beer, cheese, and other foodstuffs. In return Antwerp sent jewels, silks, quicksilver, gold, and silver thread, spices, drugs, sugar, cotton, lace, linen, tapestries, glass, armor, dried fish, household implements, and tools of war. Some of the new industries included diamond cutting and sugar refining. Five hundred ships were said to arrive in Antwerp on a single tide, while a thousand freight wagons a week rolled in from Germany, France, and other parts of the Low Countries. Antwerp's age was also the age of discovery, and the port was open to the trade of the oceans, the goods from new worlds. Traders from Scandinavia, Portugal, England, Spain, and Germany set up their headquarters in Antwerp. The English merchant-adventurers made it their northern European depot. The copper market moved there from Venice. The Antwerp Stock Exchange was dedicated *ad usum mercatorum cuiusque gentis ac linguae,* for the use of merchants of any race or language.

The Bourse, or Exchange, a remarkable building that stood from 1531 to 1581, cost some 300,000 gold crowns and had a large rectangular courtyard within and shops above the exchange where painters—close to potential patrons—sold their work. The Bourse was the heart that pumped the vital blood of the whole Hapsburg world. Monarchs borrowed there—Charles V, Philip II, and Elizabeth of England among them. (The bankers, said Pirenne, liberated the kings of that age from the embarrassing control of their subjects.) A bill on Antwerp—denoting credit for a certain sum—was the most common form of international currency. Very little coined money was needed, as the merchants preferred to give and take credit.

Such merchants as the German Fugger family, who got their start in copper and silver mines, became the Rockefellers or Rothschilds of the time. The Fuggers had their headquarters in Augsburg, but their Antwerp branch, founded in 1508, made the greatest profits. Albrecht Dürer, the German artist, remarked on Jacob Fugger's house, which he saw when visiting Antwerp: "He has newly built it in very costly fashion, with a noteworthy tower, broad and high, and with a beautiful garden." Jacob Fugger took over control of the family capital in 1511, and left assets of two million ducats when he died in 1525. His successor, Anton Fugger, left six million. The Fuggers loaned great sums

John Calvin, militant leader of the Reformation, which reshaped Dutch society
OVERLEAF: *Brueghel's "Children's Games," depicting youthful pastimes*

to Charles V, notably the fund for buying the imperial crown. Tawney writes that "after an election conducted with the publicity of an auction and the morals of a gambling hell, [the Fuggers] browbeat him, when the debt was not paid, in the tone of a pawnbroker rating a necessitous client." The Fuggers also found the money with which Charles raised the troops to fight the Protestants in 1552. "The head of the firm built a church and endowed an almshouse for the aged poor in his native town of Augsburg. He died in the odor of sanctity, a good Catholic and a Count of the Empire, having seen his firm pay 54 per cent for the preceding sixteen years." The Fuggers' road to Heaven was paved by imperial debts.

Antwerp was a crowded, lively city; some hundred thousand people lived there in 1550. Rents were high, and small houses had many people living in them. Disease, plague, and fire continued to take their regular toll. Yet in the mid-sixteenth century, boom conditions prevailed: new houses, shops, warehouses, breweries, markets, and guild-halls were constructed. In 1542 the city walls were expanded at great cost. New canals, quays, and streets were laid out. The general prosperity was evident in the richly decorated religious processions, the teeming markets, and particularly in the way the burghers lived. The Florentine Francesco Guicciardini wrote: "To enter their houses and to behold the abundance of furniture and all sorts of household implements, all equally neat and exquisite, gives one much pleasure and even greater surprise, for there is, probably, nothing in the world that equals it." A piece of furniture that was to be seen in most merchants' houses was the Flemish *kist,* a chest elegantly built, bound with wrought iron, with an elaborate lock and intricate lid designs of silver nails and gilded leatherwork. Dutch and Flemish families still have either such a chest or a *kabinet,* a combined chest and sideboard in which linen, silver, and other household valuables are kept.

A new industry that flourished in this prosperous time was that of book manufacture. Antwerp issued more than half the books printed in the Low Countries between 1510 and 1540. There were fifty printers' shops in the city. Although Aalst in the southern Low Countries and Haarlem farther north had pioneered Netherlands printing—and printers were also active in Gouda, Leiden, Delft, Utrecht, and Deventer—Antwerp soon became the headquarters of the industry.

Contemporary religious controversies fed the presses, and the presses inspired new controversies. Protestant-tinged, English-language Bibles were edited and published in Antwerp because they could not be printed in England. When Antwerp book dealers were prohibited from publishing Protestant works they turned out missals and propaganda works for the Catholic cause.

Much of the scholarly and scientific life of the Low Countries (and indeed, much of Europe) revolved around the printing firm of Plantin. Christophe Plantin was not only the leading Antwerp printer but had a branch in Leiden, run by a son-in-law; the family activities included a bookstore in the cloisters of Antwerp Cathedral, run by Plantin's wife and daughters. In his printing shop, he employed forty men and seven presses, and in the course of 34 years in Antwerp published more than 1,500 works—nearly 50 a year. (Authors did not necessarily do well from this; they sometimes got ten florins for their manuscript, while the wages of expert printers were some 140 florins a year. But more often authors were paid in free copies of the printed book, whose production costs they were also expected to help subsidize.) Plantin's great work was the Polyglot Bible, a reliable text of the testaments in Latin, Greek, Syriac, Hebrew, and Chaldean. Printing took four years. Twelve hundred copies cost the then immense sum of 100,000 florins to produce, and Plantin's financial problems were not alleviated by the fact that it took another seven years for the great book to gain church approval. One Spanish theologian denounced the work as "heretical, judaistic, the product of enemies of the church."

In the Low Countries, Guicciardini noted, "the larger part of the people have some rudiments of grammar; at any rate, nearly all, down to the peasants, can read and write." Learning and scholarship flourished in this atmosphere. In Antwerp were published Amerigo Vespucci's book of exploration and the first world atlas of Ortelius. The mapmaker, Gerhard Kremer, called Mercator, lived in nearby Rupelmonde. The new ideas of the century bloomed in this city where there was a living to be made, money to spend, and the relatively new medium of printed books to carry one's ideas and proposals across Europe. In Antwerp for a while lived Sir Thomas More, who set his *Utopia* in its gardens. More was opposed to monasticism, clerical celibacy, and the worship of relics. And perhaps the most notable literary participant in

the growing debate about religion was Erasmus of Rotterdam. Erasmus ("the first journalist," as Kenneth Clark calls him) experienced in his youth the teachings of the Brethren of the Common Life. Through his witty and caustic writings he worked for the purification of the Church —a church to be reformed of time-encrusted abuses (such as the sale of indulgences) and clerical privileges. But Erasmus was no supporter of revolution. When he heard of the first Protestant martyrs in the Low Countries he wrote: "I know not whether I must deplore their deaths or not. Certain it is that they died with great and unheard-of steadfastness, though not for the principles but the paradoxes of Luther, for which I would not be willing to die because I do not understand them."

Erasmus radiated an enlightened moderation. He wanted schools (rather than monasteries) where children would learn letters and manners and be prepared for a civilized life in this world, rather than for the next. He held an optimistic belief in the good that would come through the development of individual personalities by intelligent teaching. He wrote in 1518, "I believe I see a golden age dawning in the near future." But though Antwerp and the southern Low Countries had in terms of material prosperity something of a golden age within this half century, the true spirit of such an age, the golden spirit that moved Erasmus, was not so prevalent. What Huizinga calls the velvet softness of Erasmus was opposed by the iron hardness in the shape of Luther, on one side, and the Spanish general, Fernando Álvarez de Toledo, the duke of Alba, representative of the Spanish government, on the other.

The Protestant tide in the Low Countries rose in three main stages. First, Lutheran; second, Anabaptist; third, Calvinist. Luther, the Saxon miner's son, monk, and theology professor, attacked the papacy and the traditional organization of the Church. His radical theological proposition was that good works would not save a Christian—only faith would. But the German masses were enthusiastic about Luther not so much because of his theology but because of his attacks on the clergy and the pope. The princes saw an opportunity in this widespread zeal for sweeping away (and perhaps into their pockets) the revenues and property of the Church. On the other hand, Charles V, Holy Roman Emperor, king of Spain, and ally of the Church, felt no such

In "The Ship of Fools," Bosch limns the follies of the Catholic clergy.

enthusiasm for Luther and his cause. Unable to suppress the heretics in Germany itself—where a major religious conflict would have crippled German support for his war against Francis I of France—Charles concentrated on putting down the reform movement in the Low Countries. Although Charles' counselors opposed his introduction of the Spanish Inquisition in the Low Countries, and the pope himself protested against the lay inquisition which Charles set up instead, the prosecution of heretics proceeded. A series of drastic bills were promulgated. The emperor compelled the civil courts to sentence to death all those who—not being theologians—discussed matters of faith or any person who failed to denounce a heretic if he knew one.

This policy aroused dissent. The first martyrs of the Reformation were two Augustinians of Antwerp, Henri Voes and Jan van Esch, who on July 1, 1523, were burned alive in the Brussels market place. Luther later dedicated to them his hymn of God's miraculous works, *Brussel in Niederland.* Erasmus declared that their deaths made many Lutherans. But though this may have been the case, and though many of Luther's ideas had already been conceived in the Low Countries by Wessel Gansfort (who died in 1489), Luther's dogmas did not really take hold in the Low Countries. It was hard to convince people there that they were wrong in thinking, as they did, that doing good made you a better person and more liable to gain eternal life, if there was one. The Brethren of the Common Life had stressed the value of good works. Netherlanders found in the Scriptures (whose authority Luther proclaimed) plenty of evidence for their belief that faith alone was not enough—the Epistle of James, for instance, recommended good works as a means to a better life.

There were, for that matter, many within the Church who were working for reform, who preached the necessity of it, and whose sermons aroused great interest. In 1557 a Venetian diplomat wrote from the Netherlands, "No other people show so great a devotion in attending holy services." One of the more moderate popes of this age was Adrian of Utrecht, Charles' former teacher—the only lowlander ever to sit in the papal chair. Although the mass of people were not attracted to Lutheranism, they were particularly touched by the simple tenets of Anabaptism—a creed which came out of Germany in the 1530s and blossomed in the Low Countries. It held out the promise of a new world on earth, communal possession, and legal polygamy, but demanded strict obedience to the Word of God as expressed in the Bible. The first prophet of the creed was Melchior Hoffmann, who—having been expelled from Strasbourg—was given refuge in Amsterdam. But this sanctuary was temporary; the council of Holland found Hoffmann's activities too revolutionary and they had him decapitated. His Dutch followers then set up a new "kingdom of Zion" in Münster, where the citizens of the city had revolted against their archbishop, and an Anabaptist republic had been proclaimed. To this earthly paradise thousands of lowlanders, in a state of fanatic delirium, made their way. The poor and the downtrodden revolted in Amsterdam and Friesland; hundreds died when troops intervened. Pirenne writes, "At no other moment of history, perhaps, has there been a more striking example of the lengths to which the masses may be driven by passion, religious illusion, and the hope of realizing social justice."

After this outburst of violence the Anabaptists worked their way back to the original beliefs of the movement. Under Menno Simons (from whom the Mennonites took their name) of Witmarsum, in Friesland, they became a mild, pacific, undogmatic sect, whose members sought their individual way to God, untrammeled by institutions. The followers of Menno provided many of the martyrs of the period. Although the Protestant martyrologies suggest that some 233 people were executed for their beliefs during the reign of Charles V, historians now believe that—including those who died in the Anabaptist risings—several thousand is nearer the mark (both figures are much lower than the sensational total of thirty thousand martyrs in Holland and Friesland alone, reported by one Venetian in 1546). However, in the face of Charles' decrees many Protestants left the Low Countries at this time. From Antwerp and the coastal provinces they moved to England, and from North Holland and Friesland they went into northern Germany, to Alsace, and to Geneva, the city of John Calvin.

In the 1550s and 1560s the doctrines of Calvin began to spread through the Low Countries—first in the French-speaking southern provinces, close to the border with France, and then sweeping through the larger cities of Flanders and Brabant and on into the northern provinces. Calvin provided stern dogmas to oppose the dogmas of Rome—a militant faith to suit an increasingly militant age. For Calvin,

the state was to be an agency of Divine Will. Personal salvation in the life to come depended solely upon that Will and not on human efforts, but individuals could convince themselves that they were going to be saved by devoting themselves actively to God's service. However, this devotion was often rigorously enforced. In Geneva, heresy against Calvinist doctrines was dealt with as savagely as Calvinists elsewhere were treated by the Inquisition. Calvin got a good deal of support in the Low Countries from the merchant classes—he approved of money being lent for interest, unlike Luther, who followed the traditional teachings of the Church in this respect (though, goodness knows, there had been usury enough in medieval Flemish cities). Members of the Antwerp Stock Exchange were among the first Calvinist converts in the Low Countries. In other walks of life, Calvinism also found support. French-speaking noblemen saw in Calvin's *Institution Chrétienne* a strong argument to support their growing anxieties about the Church of

Philip II of Spain (astride) and the dukes of Alençon and Alba exploit the fat Netherlandish cow while Queen Elizabeth and William of Orange look on.

Rome. The new faith was propagated by ministers whose fervor proved contagious. The ministers recruited consistories, or cadres, of laymen, and their militant convictions seemed to spread and take hold in direct proportion to the need for secrecy forced on them, and the persecution that met them when they were found out.

Charles V's favorite painter was the Venetian artist Titian. A great portrait of Charles, painted by Titian, hangs in the Bavarian State Museum, Munich. In it Charles appears as a rather sad monarch, already, in 1548, old before his time, perhaps even then thinking about abdication and retiring to a monastery. Although he was born in Ghent, and retained an affection for his country of birth, Charles saw the Low Countries chiefly as the source of the funds by which he maintained his imperial position and financed his wars. It was a tragedy that, once again, following the Merovingians, the Carolingians, and the Burgundians, the Low Countries were ruled by a dynasty which (in Pieter Geyl's words) "never lost its alien character and always pursued objects not only foreign but inimical to the cause of the Netherlands nationality." (A point of view, of course, which assumes that there were advantages for the lowlanders in policies that encouraged cohesion and national development of all the provinces together.) Certainly neither the repression of Protestantism nor the Hapsburg wars against France had any profit in them for the Low Countries.

One group of people who prospered from the international connections of the Hapsburgs were Low Countries artists. Many painters traveled from one court to another. The brilliant portraitist Anthonis Mor of Utrecht was dispatched by Charles' sister, the Low Countries' regent, Mary of Hungary, to paint her sister, Queen Catherine of Portugal. Mor then went on to England to paint Mary Tudor for Philip II of Spain; he was given for his services an English knighthood. In the Low Countries the influence of foreign art was strongly felt at this time, and the effect of Italian painting was not perhaps always well assimilated. However, Old Testament cartoons by Raphael were sent to Brussels to be translated into tapestries, and made a wide impression, particularly on artists working in stained glass and altarpieces. The Italian influence is to be seen as well in architecture and sculpture, in the oak rood screen at Enkhuizen, the choir stalls at Dordrecht, and the antique embellishments of many civic buildings; it is also evident in needlepoint and lace—for in Flanders the pattern books of Venetian lacemakers were now in use.

Two painters who preserved a thorough Netherlandish individuality were Hieronymus Bosch and Pieter Brueghel the Elder. Although Brueghel made a trip to Italy, and mountains are depicted in his work, his style remained unaffected. Bosch (c. 1450–1516) lived and worked in the North Brabant town of 's Hertogenbosch, a name which is perhaps easier to pronounce and understand in its French form, Bois-le-Duc. In Bosch's work, however, it is sometimes hard to see the wood for the trees—detail is at once fantastic and microscopic. Medieval nightmares are shown with the precise pictorial skills of the great Low Countries illuminators. Yet the force is modern, even "Freudian." It makes acceptable the suggestions of some art historians that Bosch was a member of one of the heretical sects, a Free Spirit group perhaps. But though the clergy suspected him, his work found favor with Philip II, Charles V's son—and Philip had no love of heretics. It may be that Philip saw and admired in Bosch's work an accurate rendition of the secret cravings of man's soul, panoramas of the abyss. Many of Bosch's paintings are exotic landscapes of the grotesque, the demonic, and the perverse. They now seem to be a kind of early science fiction art, though in many cases they are based on traditional Netherlands parables and proverbs. There is also a good deal of satire in them—satire of priests and of monarchs in such paintings as "The Ship of Fools" and "The Hay Wain"; no longer the microscopic reverence of Van Eyck and Memling, but detailed horror and accurate disgust.

In both Bosch and Brueghel (c. 1525–1569), there is an element that the Low Countries painters of the fifteenth century lacked. The paintings of the earlier period are "real" enough but somewhat static. There is no notion of progress, the gradual improvement of the human species here on earth, or a sense that anything different may be expected in the future. But in Brueghel and in Bosch there is a movement —a current of disquiet. Brueghel was, like Bosch, a North Brabant man; the village of Brueghel is not far from 's Hertogenbosch. Pieter Brueghel served his apprenticeship in Antwerp, married the daughter of his teacher Pieter Coeck van Aelst, and moved to Brussels in 1563. His surviving paintings were produced in a mere eleven years, 1558–1569. In them, the popular life of the time is portrayed, and for as long as those paintings last we will have a tangible witness to the Low Countries in the mid-sixteenth century: to fields and villages in various seasons, under snow or at harvest time, and to the way the common people lived. Men drink, work, and hunt; children play. There are peasant festivals and weddings. There is war and death.

Brueghel painted numerous works that have ostensibly Biblical subjects—for example, "The Massacre of the Innocents" and "The Census of Bethlehem." In them troops and officials look more Spanish than Roman, more Philip's than Herod's. Brussels in the late 1560s was garrisoned by Spanish troops under the duke of Alba. Rebellion and heresy were being stamped out with fire and sword. Brueghel left instructions that some of his last drawings be destroyed after his death; he had written remarks on them that he was afraid would get his wife in trouble. Even so, his work like that of Bosch found favor with the Hapsburgs, which is why much of it is to be seen now in Madrid and Vienna. Yet Brussels retains one of Brueghel's most characteristic paintings, "The Fall of Icarus." In this work Icarus is hardly seen— there is a small splash in the lower, right-hand corner, and two legs disappearing beneath the green water of a bay. Regardless of the foolhardy aviator, who was so ambitious to improve the means of human transport, a galleon sails by, a man fishes from a rocky cliff overlooking the bay, a shepherd (somewhat asleep on his feet) takes care of his sheep, and a farmer steers his plow along a winding furrow with age-old concentration on the task at hand. The moral of the picture seems to be that whatever happens, great events or small, life goes on.

CHAPTER V

REVOLT OF THE NETHERLANDS

During a ceremony in Brussels in 1555, Charles V, worn out and crippled with gout, handed over the Low Countries and Spain to his son Philip. It was a moving scene: Charles, born in Ghent, still aroused feelings of loyalty, despite his heavy handed government. He appeared before the assembled States General, leaning on the young William of Orange, surrounded by his Knights of the Golden Fleece. He said that he had always acted from a sense of duty, not ambition, in his exercise of imperial power. He wept, and the assembled company wept too. He then retired to a Spanish monastery, where he died three years later.

Unfortunately for the Low Countries, Philip II acted like more of a Spaniard than his father had. He spoke neither French nor Dutch. After 1559, although he reigned for nearly forty more years, he never set foot in the Low Countries. If the nicknaming tradition of the Burgundian dukes had continued, Philip might well have been called Philip the Foreigner. Under his rule the great wealth of the provinces was drained away; the southern Netherlands, including Antwerp, was ruined; and the fragile unity of the region was shattered.

It was clear that, despite the centralizing policy of the Burgundians

Jacob van Ruisdael depicts bolts of cloth spread out to dry in the foreground of his view of Haarlem, trading center of Holland in the seventeenth century.

and Hapsburgs, the Low Countries were still in many respects a collection of separate provinces in which the center of gravity had shifted a little north by east, from Flanders to Brabant, from Bruges and Ghent to Brussels and Antwerp. The northern provinces were still generally poorer. In the 1490s the northern peasants had revolted against the government, attacking law officers and tax collectors. During the Hapsburg wars, particularly in the long struggle over Gelderland, many northern towns were looted by troops and the countryside laid waste. The Zuider Zee was often unsafe, with Frisian privateers plundering valuable cargoes. Yet in the province of Holland, from the middle of the sixteenth century, agricultural and urban prosperity rapidly increased. Guicciardini remarked on the amount of butter and cheese, and the great numbers of horses and cattle. Efforts were being made to reclaim more land from the sea—to which large areas had been lost in the great floods of 1509, 1530, and 1532. (Charles V had observed the successful fund-raising methods of the Church and had promoted an "indulgence" to collect maintenance funds for the dikes. However, Erasmus claimed that none of the money went to that project.)

Holland had begun to feel that it was a special place. In a petition to Charles V, the States Assembly of Holland said: "It is noticeable that the province of Holland is only a small country, not very long and still less wide, enclosed by the sea on three sides. It must be protected against the sea by dikes . . . sluices, mills and moats. Moreover, it contains many dunes, moors, and inland waters, which grow more extensive day by day, barren lands unfit for fields or pastures." The States General—which in this period developed into an official, institutional voice for the province—explained that therefore the people of the country were involved in shipping, fishing, and related trades dealing with salt and timber, hemp and tar. Holland and Zeeland sent some six hundred ships a year to the fishing grounds, with roughly twenty men on each ship and numerous shore workers and their families dependent on the business. It was with good reason that one writer in 1577 called the herring *Gratia Dei*, "for people make this their daily food far more than any other fish. . . . We might as well call these fisheries the Golden Mountain or the Triumph of Holland."

Philip II inherited many problems with his Low Countries domains. The long wars and heavy tax demands had created much discontent.

The finances of the provinces were in confusion, the high nobility were intractable and the States General, with delegates from the various provincial assemblies, insisted that the three thousand Spanish troops leave the land now that the Low Countries forces had helped Spain defeat the French. Philip's establishment of new bishoprics for qualified theologians annoyed wealthy abbots and great lords who were used to putting some of their unqualified sons in bishops' jobs. Dissent was intensified by the rivalries between towns and countryside over industrial labor and the rights of taxation; by the competition between one town and another; and—within the towns—by the struggles between the guilds and the oligarchies which controlled the town councils. The lawyers and government officials in Brussels antagonized the country gentry, who had been accustomed to administering justice and looking after their own petty spheres of influence. Bernard Vlekke, the Dutch historian, writes: "By the middle of the XVIth century there was enough inflammable material in the Low Countries to set the whole country ablaze, even without the great spiritual conflict that divided the people into two violently opposed camps."

In the matter of religion, Philip made no concessions. He reinforced his father's repressive edicts and as a result political discontent and religious unrest were further aroused and added their collective com-

An enterprising Dutch trader, holding his wife's hand, points with pride to the fleet of the East India Company, anchored in the bay of Batavia, Java.

bustive force to the flame. Although the Calvinists were still only a tiny minority, many ordinary Catholics resented the Inquisition. Often the judges themselves were openly doubtful of the rightness of the law they had to administer. Sheriffs and executioners went in danger of assassination. In 1565 a league of the lower nobility formed to demand a redress of grievances; they condemned the Inquisition as "contrary to all laws human and divine." They represented the rising tide of popular feeling against the Hapsburg government. A year later, in April, 1566, three hundred nobles from almost every province of the Low Countries made a solemn procession to the Brussels palace of the regent, Philip's sister Margaret, the duchess of Parma, who had been entrusted with administering the region. They handed her a petition for the king in Spain. Legend has it that one of her counselors, trying to reassure her, told her not to be frightened of "these beggars."

The term "beggars" stuck—indeed the rebellious nobles treated it as a title of honor. Soon it served as a *nom de guerre* for bands in Flanders—the Wild Beggars—and squadrons of coastal freebooters— the Sea Beggars. Although the duchess made temporary concessions, the discontent grew, increased by a failure of bread supplies. In the countryside, there was an epidemic of public preaching by the Calvinists. At these open-air services (to quote the chronicler Willem van Haecht), "the women sat in the middle inside a circle marked out with stakes and cords; their servants and soldiers, who kept guard, formed fighting order after the sermon, and then they fired stray shots and now and then would shout 'Long live the beggars!' At Ghent the assemblies outside the town were commonly twenty thousand strong. . . . So it was throughout almost all Flanders, Holland, and Zeeland."

The wave of fury crested and broke in August, 1566, as crowds of frenzied people raided the churches in one community after another, destroying statues, paintings, vestments, and carvings. The clergy went into hiding. The iconoclasts declared that they were taking revenge on the idols for all the living creatures destroyed by the Inquisition. But shortly revenge was taken on the rebels. Hundreds were executed, and many dissenters, previously sympathetic but now suddenly aware of how savage the Calvinists could be too, rallied to the duchess of Parma. Many Calvinists went into exile, including William I of Orange, the governor of Holland, Zeeland, and Utrecht, who now retired for the moment to his German estates. Perhaps the duchess would have done well now on her own. But Philip sent in the duke of Alba, Fernando Álvarez de Toledo, with ten thousand Spanish and Italian troops. A reign of blood began.

The duke, who thought Holland was close to the Inferno, set about making the entire Low Countries a veritable Hell on earth. The counts of Egmont and Hoorn, two of the leading opposition noblemen, were arrested. A special court, soon nicknamed the Blood Council, was established to try all those suspected of rebellion. Alba reported to his king in January, 1568: "A great deal remains to be done first. The towns must be punished for their rebelliousness . . . a goodly sum must be squeezed out of private persons; a tax obtained from the States of the country. It would therefore be unsuitable to proclaim a pardon at this juncture. Everyone must be made to live in constant fear. . . ."

The estates of refugees were seized, numerous arrests were made, and on June 5, in the Great Market Square of Brussels, Egmont and Hoorn were beheaded. Within the year Alba had prepared a stringent 1 per cent property tax and a 10 per cent sales tax—a Low Countries version of the Spanish *alcabala*. The States General had been cowed and many of the nobility were begging humble forgiveness.

A leader against Alba had, however, fortunately appeared in the exiled William of Orange. Prince William's mother was a Lutheran, and although he had been brought up as a Catholic, he rejoined the Lutheran faith in 1566 and became a Calvinist in 1573. But he was not a fanatic; he acted out of practical policy and in the spirit of Erasmian moderation, always trying to keep the opposition to the Spanish from becoming one-sidedly Calvinist—he knew that he would get more support from other monarchs of Europe if Calvinism was played down. (In 1566 William gave advice to the duchess of Parma while at the same time he was collecting troops to oppose her.) He proclaimed the principle that the sovereign (in this case Philip) had no absolute power over his subjects; his power ceased to be legal when it encroached upon their ancient charters and local privileges. "The privileges are not free grants of the sovereign to his subjects, but firm contracts binding both prince and people." Yet William's attempt to invade the Low Countries in 1568 was easily thwarted by Alba.

William attempted without much success to get aid from the Ger-

A painting of 1614, showing Protestants and Catholics competing for souls on

opposite banks of a river, symbolizes the bitter religious schisms in Europe.

man Protestant princes and the French Huguenots for an invasion in 1572, and the war of liberation was given its first real boost by native rebels. This was the attack and capture of the Maas River port of Brielle, on April 1, 1572, by a squadron of the Sea Beggars (the name given to the corsairs of all nationalities who were currently devastating the coast and coastal shipping). They had captured some 300 ships, taken vast quantities of booty, and had 84 ships of their own by April, 1570. They performed bloody atrocities, slaughtering monks, priests, and Catholic magistrates, and though anti-Spanish, brought little honor to the Calvinist cause. William was upset by their cruelty and the disrepute they attached to him as a result of their actions—and also by the fact that no share of the booty ever reached him. He attempted to regulate their behavior by giving them letters of marque, but to little avail. However, in 1572 Queen Elizabeth of England revoked the tacit permission she had given for the Beggars to use English ports and the Beggars willy-nilly were forced to act more positively in the Orange cause. A fleet of 28 under the Beggar commanders Lumey de la Marck and Blois van Treslong was driven by strong westerly winds to take refuge in the Maas estuary. Anchored off Brielle, they found the Spanish garrison had marched off to Utrecht to help quell a disturbance. So the 600-strong band of Beggars marched in, pillaged the churches, murdered Catholic officials, and collected booty, but—contrary to their usual practice—stayed, perhaps because they had no other port to sail to. The inhabitants took the oath to the stadholder. The flag of the prince of Orange flew over Brielle, and the Beggars successfully held the town against a Spanish relief expedition. The Scheldt River port of Vlissingen added momentum to the revolt by calling in the Beggars a few days later. At once town after town began to cast off its allegiance to Spain. William of Orange was their man. Exiles streamed back into the Low Countries, joining the three-pronged invasion led by the prince, his brother Louis of Nassau, and his brother-in-law Count Van den Berg. But their victories were not extensive. Louis was defeated. William, short of money to pay his troops, was forced to retrench against Alba's ferocious armies in what was to become the heartland of the revolt, the provinces of Holland and Zeeland.

The war lasted more than a generation. New leaders came and went. But the fighting ended earlier in the southern provinces. Geography had a hand here, for one element which preserved the north was water —as the Sea Beggars showed, the men of Holland and Zeeland were great seamen—and the northern rivers were obstacles to the Spanish armies. The troops of Alba and his son Don Frederick devastated Malines, Zutphen, and Naarden—rape, murder, and arson were the fate of each—but it took the Spanish seven months to capture Haarlem in 1573. This was the long, slow turning point. It encouraged the rebels and made the Spanish wonder if they had bitten off more than they could chew. Later that same year, at Alkmaar, the Spanish forces were repulsed. Leiden held out against an obstinate Spanish siege, and the prince of Orange honored its success by founding a university there— it was a note of confidence in the future. On the newly minted coins issued by the municipal government of Leiden during the siege it said, *Haec Libertatis Ergo* (All This for Freedom's Sake).

One of Leiden's ministers, the Reverend Adriaan Taling, complained that the motto should have been All This for Religion's Sake; but despite this, and despite that fact that Calvinism was encouraged to take hold as proof of the break with Catholic Spain, many felt at the time that they were indeed fighting for their old privileges and freedoms; they felt that laws and decrees should be enforced with moderation. Probably most did not question the right of the government to put down heresy, but they did object strongly to the way the government did so, with bloody executions and confiscations.

It was not an age of great cultural activity. The Italianate Classical style still dominated in architecture and painting, and writing was heavily impressed with the artificial conventions of the Chambers of Rhetoric. Original talents were few, but they include Philippe de Marnix, lord of Saint Aldegonde, a Calvinist noble who retired from the contemporary uproar to his country estate in Zeeland, where he translated the Bible, published a scathingly satirical attack on Catholicism, *Beehive of the Holy Roman Church* (1570), and produced a superb Dutch version of the Psalms. Then there was Hendrik Spieghel, Catholic merchant and Rhetorician of Amsterdam, but a man of great tolerance and imagination, and author of *Mirror of the Heart.* Spieghel and his colleagues tried in 1585 to persuade Leiden University to give its courses in Dutch rather than Latin, though they had no success. Perhaps the true spirit of the age came through most clearly in the

Beggars' Songs, anonymous ballads which quickly passed from town to town. The author is also unknown of the *Wilhelmas,* a ballad written about 1568, in which William of Orange is made to proclaim his fervent attachment to his land and—in what was a bad moment—encourage his countrymen to look for comfort if not in this life, then in the life to come. In this hymn William emphasizes his loyalty to Philip—he was a rebel against bad government, not against his king. The *Wilhelmas* is the Dutch national anthem:

> *Unto the Lord His power*
> *I do confession make*
> *That ne'er at any hour*
> *Ill of the King I spake.*
> *But unto God, the greatest*
> *Of Majesties, I owe*
> *Obedience first and latest,*
> *For justice wills it so.*

After the siege of Leiden in 1574 the war is best examined in two stages. The first runs from 1575 to 1585, a decade marked at the beginning by the Spanish Fury in Antwerp and at the end by Antwerp's capitulation to the Spanish after a year-long struggle. In November, 1575, the unpaid Spanish troops were in a state of angry mutiny; they marched from their encampment, joined the guards from the Antwerp citadel, and set fire to the town. Seven thousand people were killed, five hundred houses were destroyed, and the Spanish soldiers spent three weeks loading up the booty they had stolen from the city in lieu of their pay. (Although Alba had gone, replaced by the more moderate governor, Luis de Zúñiga y Requeséns, the Spanish were still faced with insuperable financial problems.) But the reaction to the "Fury" unleased by the Spanish on Antwerp helped bring about a temporary union of the Low Countries. In a treaty called the Pacification of Ghent (November 8, 1576), the provinces agreed (at least on paper) that they would combine to expel the Spanish. Because the Catholic lowlanders needed the militant backing of the Calvinists, they agreed to terms that were not so favorable to themselves. Calvinist practices were to be allowed in the south and religious questions were to be

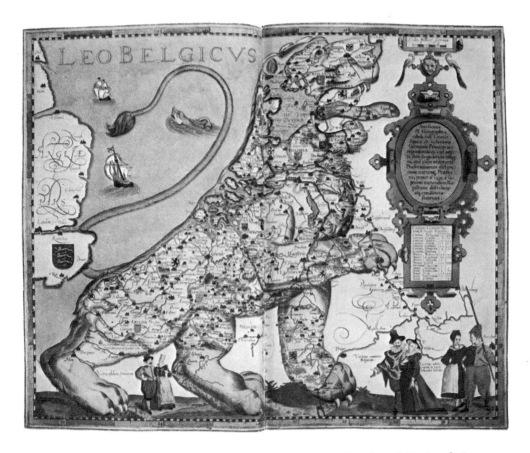

settled by the States General. In the north, in Holland and Zeeland, it was implicitly recognized that the Calvinists were in charge.

From this point, the war began to go their way. Don Juan of Austria, the romantic general Philip next sent in as governor, had to wait in Luxembourg until he accepted the terms of the Pacification. The Spanish troops were forced to leave the country. And thus for a time William of Orange triumphed. At Brussels he made a Joyous Entry, the procession marking the inauguration of a reign. He was greeted by poet-orators, guards of honor, and the cheers of the people.

But the celebrations were premature. Don Juan soon denounced the Pacification and called back the Spanish troops; this treachery threw into confusion the party of high Catholic nobility who had supported Don Juan, and underlined the good sense that William had shown when he continued to distrust the Spanish intentions. The lines of hatred and enmity were now being deeply drawn. In January, 1578, Don Juan's soldiers won a considerable victory at Gembloux against

In Pieter van der Keere's 1617 map, the lion of the Netherlands fights for independence from Spain, roars defiance at Europe, and flicks its tail at England.

the States General's troops. The Calvinists then proceeded to occupy Catholic monasteries and to empty the churches of their decorations, even to the extent of whitewashing the interior walls. Although William preached moderation, his words could control neither the Calvinist drive nor the fierce Catholic reaction to it. Walloons fought Flemings, while Alexander Farnese, duke of Parma (Don Juan's successor), allowed his forces to maraud Brabant.

In the next few years the revolt suffered considerably. Spanish-held Luxembourg, together with Namur, Limburg, and part of Hainaut, formed a solid Catholic bastion for Philip II. The rest of the Walloon French-speaking provinces now quit the Orange cause; and together they formed a Union of Arras and made their peace with the duke of Parma. John of Nassau, William's brother, brought about a Union of Utrecht, but this was signed by only the northern representatives of Gelderland, Holland, Zeeland, and Utrecht. Friesland, Overijssel, and Drenthe declared their somewhat less than unanimous sympathy. At this time Amsterdam finally put aside profits for provincial patriotism and came over to the Orangist camp. Priests and monks were driven out and the merchant poet Hendrik Spieghel wrote of the Calvinists:

> *They who at first asked for no more than to live in freedom,*
> *Now have their liberty, but will not give it to others.*

As Catholics everywhere became antagonized by the increasingly intolerant Calvinist regimes, Parma continued to win battles.

In 1580 Philip proscribed the man, who twenty-five years before had supported Philip's father at his abdication ceremony. He denounced William of Orange as "chief perturber and corrupter of entire Christianity and especially of the Netherlands." A reward of 25,000 golden crowns, plus patents of nobility, was offered to anyone who produced the rebel prince dead or alive. William replied in an eloquent *Apologia*, reviewing his life and deeds: "The mischief has all arisen from the cruelty and arrogance of the Spaniard, who thinks he can make slaves of us, as if we were Indians or Italians. . . . I was bred a Catholic and a worldling, but the horrible persecution that I witnessed and the plot to introduce worse than Spanish Inquisition . . . made me resolve in my soul to rest not until I had chased from the land these locusts of Spain."

William scoffed at Philip's assassins—"Does he think he can ennoble my assassin? If this be the road to nobility in Castile, there is not a gentleman in the world, among nations that know what is true nobility, who would hold converse with so cowardly a miscreant."

In 1581 the States General at The Hague formally renounced their allegiance to Philip of Spain, declaring that a prince was ordained for the well-being of his people—not the people for the well-being of the prince. Brave words; but the rebels' problems got worse. The Orange troops were underpaid and mutinous, and Parma's forces raided everywhere except in Holland and Zeeland, which were protected by their rivers and inundated fields. The oppression of the Catholics by the Calvinists undermined the position of Francis of Alençon, the French duke of Anjou and a Catholic, to whom the States, with Orange's prodding, had offered their allegiance after withdrawing it from Philip. William wanted to use Anjou's influence to promote the French alliance, and perhaps get the French into war with Spain; but these crafty tactics disaffected many Flemings. Furthermore, Parma's policy of moderation won friends. The Inquisition was not allowed to return to the Low Countries. Calvinists were given a choice of submitting to Catholicism or moving to the northern provinces. Catholics, and indeed many of the Reformed, lost their enthusiasm for the rule of demagogues and extremists of either sect. Then, on July 10, 1584, William was assassinated in Delft—shot by one of King Philip's supporters, a Burgundian, Balthasar Gérard, who was caught, tortured, and disemboweled alive before having his heart thrown in his face. The reward was paid to his heirs. The rebel resistance in the southern provinces became halfhearted: Bruges, Ypres, Ghent, Brussels, and Malines surrendered one by one. In 1585, after a year's siege by Parma's army, Antwerp—the chief stronghold of the revolt in the south—capitulated. From this point the southern provinces were Spain's; the north was on its own.

The second stage of this critical period of Low Countries history thus begins with the provinces divided. It is from this date that the firm shape of the two modern nations of Holland and Belgium starts to appear—though nationalist historians of both countries have always been able to discern "Belgians" and "Dutchmen" in the mistiest reaches of the past. The Dutch Republic rises as Antwerp falls, with the Zeeland Sea Beggar fleet controlling the approaches to the Scheldt,

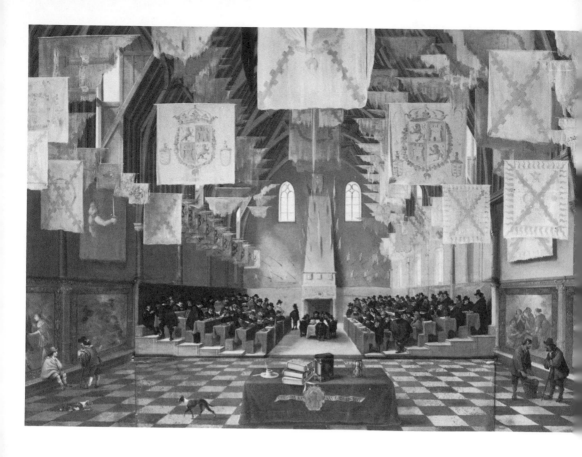

and the duke of Parma, for all his military genius, unable to do anything about it. Thousands of Antwerp's citizens left the city, some for reasons of religion (they were given four years in which to make their departure), many because with trade at a standstill they no longer had any means of making a living. Antwerp's loss was Zeeland's, Holland's, and particularly Amsterdam's gain. The refugees brought to the north their skills, their energy, and their wealth. (Much of the Flemish clothmaking trade moved to Leiden and Haarlem.) The south was left to stagnate. Antwerp's Stock Exchange became a library. However, obedience to the rule of Spain brought to the southern provinces most of their old privileges—for example, no one could be arrested without warrant from a judge, property could not be confiscated arbitrarily, and the provincial States had to consent before the central government could levy taxes. Moreover, toward the end of the century, the southern provinces developed a sort of autonomy under Philip's daughter Isabella and her husband Albert, archduke of Austria. (Philip had handed

The States General convenes in 1651 in The Hague's Hall of Knights, the impressive seat of government for the United Provinces.

over his Low Countries possessions to them on the wily condition that Spain would get them back again if their marriage proved childless.)

The vital spark had gone north, and was embodied in two men: Johan van Oldenbarneveldt, Lord Advocate of the province of Holland, and Maurice of Nassau, William of Orange's son. Oldenbarneveldt acted as spokesman and legal adviser of the nobles' delegation to the States Assembly of Holland. First to vote, and the man in charge of the agenda, he had great power. In 1585 he sailed to England to offer to Elizabeth the sovereignty of the Low Countries, forfeited by Philip and relinquished by the duke of Anjou. Elizabeth also felt threatened by Spain, but at this point she was not willing to annoy Philip by accepting the Dutch offer. She did (for a high price) send help in the form of six thousand men under the earl of Leicester. However, Leicester made one mistake after another; he chose Utrecht for his headquarters, slighting Holland, which felt it was pulling most of the weight in the fight with Spain. Leicester's troops were poorly equipped and badly trained. Leicester himself seemed more interested in taking over as lord of the Netherlands. Meanwhile, Parma continued to win successes in the field. It was a relief for Oldenbarneveldt when Leicester returned to England in 1587 and The Hague became the undisputed seat of government. There the States General met in nearly continuous session and one of the two stadholders (who in this case was not only stadholder of Holland but also of Zeeland, Gelderland, Utrecht, and Overijssel) kept his residence.

The preservation of the northern Netherlands confederation was due to this and other factors. As said, Parma's armies were held up by the rivers and lakes delimiting the northern provinces. Philip, moreover, had now embarked on his giant, deluded enterprise to seize Elizabeth's throne, and Parma had to be ready to assist the Armada. And, perhaps the most important of all factors, the northern provinces had going for them the military abilities of Maurice of Nassau. After his father's assassination, Maurice had been appointed stadholder of five of the seven provinces (his cousin William Louis of Nassau was stadholder of the other two, Groningen and Friesland). Maurice therefore—though subordinate to the States of Holland—represented the unity of the allied provinces. He reorganized the confederation's army, which was mostly made up of German soldiers of fortune. He reduced the size of the army and saw that those who remained were paid regularly, and that they were well fed and housed. He thus made the army more of a danger to the enemy and less of a threat to its employers. Rigid discipline was enforced. He introduced new skills of military engineering, made the soldiers do their own digging, improved methods of siege warfare, and cleverly used the rivers and waterways to dispatch troops for quick actions. In the campaigns of 1590 and subsequent years he recovered much of the north. On one occasion Maurice recaptured a town after the Spanish had gone into winter quarters—thinking the year's campaigns were over.

By no means a background aspect of the success of the northern United Provinces was their prosperity. "In the command of the sea and in the conduct of the war on the water resides the entire prosperity of the country," declared the States of Holland in 1596. In the midst of war the Hollanders went on trading by sea even with the Spanish. (This was one cause of their disagreement with Leicester.) Now that Antwerp was effectively shut off from maritime commerce, and the southern Calvinist merchants had emigrated north, the fleets of Zeeland, Holland, and the IJssel River towns enjoyed boom years. In 1590 Dutch merchant ships passed for the first time into the Mediterranean, following in the wake of the medieval Frisian merchantmen. Shipbuilding yards flourished. The Dutch began to take over the trade of the Portuguese in the Indies—in 1595 three ships reached Java, and when they returned to Amsterdam two years later laden with pepper and other spices they were welcomed with peals of church bells. More ships ventured in the new trade, and, with Oldenbarneveldt's prodding, the Dutch East India Company was formed in 1602. In the same years Dutch ships sailed across the Atlantic smuggling goods to and from Portuguese Brazil. Henry Hudson, an Englishman in the employ of the East India Company, sailed up the river that now bears his name. In this opening up of brave new worlds, this expansive, adventurous time, exiles from the southern Low Countries played a notable part.

In 1609 a truce was concluded with the Spanish by the States General of the republic. Although peace was not actually signed until 1648, the truce had the effect of inaugurating a new era in the northern Netherlands. It was not altogether peaceful; frontier raids on the south by the northerners continued, and in the north there was much internal

strife. The more zealous Calvinists were upset by the truce. They
wanted war to go on until the southern provinces were freed. Moreover, Prince Maurice was annoyed because his military career had not
yet been crowned with ultimate victory over the Spanish. But the
majority of the rich burghers realized that trade and prosperity were
best served by the truce. And there was no doubt that, ultimate victory
or not, the truce was a great success for the northern provinces. They
had in a generation-long war battled to a standstill the most powerful
monarchy in the world. They continued to hold the mouths and lower
courses of the Scheldt, the Maas, and the Rijn, leaving Antwerp and
the rest of Brabant and Flanders bottled up, half dead.

Yet in terms of the entire Low Countries the truce sealed the tragedy
of division—not simply a division of regions but a division of those
who shared a language. Although they regained many of their ancient
rights, most of the Dutch-speaking Spanish Netherlanders were left
below the Scheldt, along with their French-speaking countrymen, with
no defensible borders, and very much at the mercy of the power struggle that the Austrian and Spanish Hapsburgs continued to wage with
France. For that matter, within the Dutch Republic and the newly
defined Spanish Netherlands the split had the effect of polarizing the
prevailing religious tendencies. In the north, psalm singing and preaching broadcast the news that the Reformed were the new chosen people
and it was best to choose to join them. Catholic priests were given the
chance to become (and often intimidated into becoming) Calvinist
ministers. Occasionally, they were ordered to marry their housekeepers;
sometimes they refused. Reformed schools were established and education used to impose the new religion upon a people who had remained
for the most part Catholic. Geyl writes: "It is evident that the majority
of the North Netherlandish people have abandoned Catholicism under
the pressure of public authority." In the south, the process was re-
versed. Calvinists left for the north; abbeys and churches were rebuilt;
and, thrust forward by the forces of the Counter Reformation, capable
men were installed in ecclesiastical posts, high and low. The Catholic
majority in the south pulled itself together and put its war-devastated
houses and farms back in shape. Their hope to be left undisturbed was
expressed on the nameboards they commonly hung in front of their
roadside inns: *Op Hoop van Vrede,* In the Hope of Peace.

CHAPTER VI

FIRE AND
IMAGINATION

The first three quarters of the seventeenth century in the Netherlands traditionally bears the name The Golden Age. But the remarks
of the Dutch historian Johan Huizinga should be repeated: "If our
great age must perforce be given a name, let it be that of wood and
steel, pitch and tar, color and ink, pluck and piety, fire and imagination. The term 'golden' applies far better to the eighteenth century,
when our coffers were stuffed with gold-pieces." The great age is also
spanned by the life of Rembrandt, who was born in 1606, three years
before the beginning of the truce with Spain, and who died in 1669.

To our eyes the period before the truce is full of religious and military conflict and is dominated by battles and generals. The Golden Age
of the seventeenth century is crammed with economic success, exploration and maritime endeavor, with colonizing and the making of an
urban civilization in which science, the arts, and the art of toleration
were great beneficiaries. It is an amazing thing—and it amazed foreign
contemporaries as much as it amazes us now—that suddenly, out of a
somewhat lackluster past, emerged a new state, the Netherlands, completely overshadowing its southern sister; a state which was to be for

*Sturdy, hard-working burghers of Amsterdam partake of a sumptuous repast
in this detail from Frans Hals' "Banquet of the Officers of Saint George," 1616.*

seventy-five years the most powerful nation in the world. The war with Spain called forth from this small straggle of watery provinces an extraordinary upsurge of creative energy.

The northern, or United, provinces had in this period roughly one and a half million people. Of these, more than half lived in Holland and Zeeland. Holland, with some 600,000 citizens, was even then an urban area. A ring of towns ran from Dordrecht through Rotterdam, Delft, The Hague, Leiden, Haarlem, and Zaandam, to Amsterdam—whose population was over a hundred thousand. Dordrecht made linen thread while Delft had adopted the relatively new Italian craft of tin-glazed faience. In Amsterdam all kinds of industries thrived, particularly the handling of grain for much of Europe. The poet-diplomat Constantijn Huyghens called his city "the golden swamp."

In that wet, low-lying land, cities like Amsterdam were turned into tightly packed zones of relative dryness, with houses built on mounds or on piles driven into the boggy ground. Canals which drained the land also provided efficient thoroughfares for the carriage of goods and people. In most towns there were as many canals as streets, the canals planned in concentric or grid patterns, with brick houses and warehouses overlooking them and reflected in their brown waters. Narrow town houses made good use of the confined space, rising three or four stories over a storage vault at water level, often with embellished pediments and gables climbing in steps and curves. Shutters were painted in bright reds, greens, and browns. Lime and elm trees planted along the canal banks held the wet soil together with their roots and added the color of their leaves. Streets were often named after the goods to be bought there—Cheese Street and Spice Street; and the wealthier canals in Amsterdam—Keizersgracht, Prinsengracht, and Herrengracht—suggested greater ambitions. But in humbler quarters you could find the house of a pastry cook by the painted sign of an oven or of Saint Nicholas or Saint Osbert, saints associated with food. A scissors or picture of Saint Martin tearing his cloak advertised a tailor, while surgeons displayed a red, white, and blue pole—the blue for shaving, the white for pulling teeth, and the red for letting blood.

The low skyline of the town, as you can see in paintings such as those of Meindert Hobbema and Jacob van Ruisdael, was commanded by churches, guildhalls, and belfries, from which, as for ages past, bells rang at all hours in chimes and changes. The great square belfry at Zierikzee was intended to be the world's highest tower, and though it remained unfinished it was imposing enough. Saint Bavo's at Haarlem, an immense cathedral, is still to be seen; the nave of Utrecht Cathedral collapsed after a storm on August 1, 1674. The Calvinists continued their drive to "purify" the interiors of Catholic churches: statues and stained glass were removed and walls whitewashed. The minister's pulpit replaced the high altar as the center of attention. The fashion— at least for the first half of the century—was austerity. Ministers pronounced firmly against long hair for men or jewelry for women. But churches also became less special—they were now places for concerts and meetings, covered streets as it were where you could walk around, dryshod, in bad weather.

Urban life presented urban problems, and the seventeenth-century Dutch were not immune to difficulties we may think of as particular to our own time. Overcrowding was common. Speculators turned houses into slum apartments with high rents. In many towns traffic was intense. Because carriages quickly became fashionable and the streets were too narrow to accommodate their numbers, Amsterdam was forced in 1615 to adopt a one-way system around the bread market. In 1634 the municipal corporation pronounced a soon-modified ban against private carriages within the city limits—modified because the ban was felt most by the wealthy and influential. The numerous hog-backed bridges over the canals formed obstacles that freight sleds could negotiate more safely than wagons. These sleds became familiar sights, with the driver scurrying alongside putting greased rags under the runners to ease their way or throwing straw in front to bring the sled to a halt. Pedestrians were at the mercy of these unhandy contraptions, which went unlit at night.

Through the night gatekeepers and guards watched the towns. The gates were locked at a certain hour, the streets patrolled, drunkards seen home, and suspected thieves pursued. Jean Nicolas Parival, a Frenchman who taught at Leiden University, wrote of one gentleman in The Hague who, after a drinking session, killed a night watchman. But he was subject to common justice, and was beheaded, though he made appeals and proffered bribes. Despite this example, many municipal police were thought to be corrupt. Paul Zumthor, a French his-

torian, writes in his *Daily Life in Rembrandt's Holland:* "Some towns
sold the post of police chief to the highest bidder, and there was no
lack of candidates." The power to levy fines assured great fortunes.

Cleanliness was already a conspicuous compulsion. Willem Us-
selincx, a merchant and entrepreneur who became an expatriate in
Sweden when his ambitions at home were frustrated, said that at least in
Sweden he "could live in peace without being constantly disturbed by
the female mania for cleaning and dusting." Sir William Temple, the
observant British ambassador, thought that the reason for this passion
for scrubbing, dusting, carpet beating, and sweeping was the wet and
the crowdedness. "The extreme moisture of the air I take to be the occasion of the great neatness of their houses, and cleanliness in their
towns. For without the help of those customs, their country would
not be habitable by such crowds of people, but the air would corrupt
upon every hot season, and expose the inhabitants to general and in-
fectious diseases."

Frequent epidemics hit hardest the overcrowded and undernour-
ished. All manner of disease passed under the dire name of Plague—
and plague struck often. In one year thirteen thousand died in Leiden.
Every few years a town would lose as many as a quarter or a third of
its population in an epidemic; cemeteries were rarely big enough.
Smallpox, scurvy, and malaria were common. So too were such pre-
ventive and curative remedies as cow's urine and spiders' heads. But
though superstition remained deep-rooted—despite the preaching of
the Reformed—the Netherlands was in the vanguard of medical progress. The teachings of Andreas Vesalius, the celebrated sixteenth-
century anatomist of Louvain, formed an enlightened background for
experiment. The physician Jacob Swammerdam got permission from
the Amsterdam municipal council to dissect corpses. Public lectures in
anatomy were held, and were popular. Rembrandt and other artists re-
corded the performances of such eminent physicians as Dr. Nicholas
Tulp. Dr. Tulp, who became a burgomaster of Amsterdam, visited his
patients by carriage, a novelty in that age. His selfless dedication was
evident in his motto: "In serving I consume myself." A generation
later came the great Hermann Boerhaave, who devoted his life to
medical research and taught at Leiden University. His reputation was
wide. Dr. Johnson wrote after Boerhaave's death (in 1738) that he

*Pieter Saenredam's painting of Saint Bavo's church, a former Catholic edifice
whitewashed and reconverted for the use of Haarlem's Calvinists*

was "a Man formed by Nature for great Designs, and guided by Religion in the Exertion of his abilities."

Into the bustling towns of seventeenth-century Holland came people not only from the southern provinces but other countries. Portuguese and Spanish Jews, the Sephardim, took refuge particularly in Amsterdam. Jewish immigrants had more religious freedom than the Calvinist authorities allowed the Catholics or other non-Reformed Christian sects. Opposite the Montelbaan tower in Amsterdam the Jews built a copy of Solomon's temple—a galleried, triple-naved synagogue which every Saturday was packed with five or six thousand worshipers. The Ashkenazic Jews from Germany added their numbers to the Sephardic community after the outbreak of the Thirty Years' War. The Jews were barred from public office and craft guilds, so their energies often went into trade and scholarship. From France, waves of Huguenots arrived, forming their own Christian congregations and opening their own schools. They introduced new methods of clockmaking, taught the violin and the art of cooking, and served as officers and soldiers in the Dutch army—all the while complaining about the climate, the temperament of the natives, and the impossibility of the Dutch language. They took several generations to get used to the Dutch way of life. In 1685 one Frenchman reckoned that half the total population with permanent abodes in the province of Holland were foreigners or their immediate descendants.

The civil wars and religious troubles that plagued France, Germany, and England through the seventeenth century increased (in Sir William Temple's eloquent words) "the swarm in this Country, not only by such as were persecuted at home, but great numbers of peaceable men, who came here to seek for quiet in their Lives, and safety in their Possessions or Trades; like those Birds that upon the approach of a rough Winter season, leave the Countrys where they were born and bred, flye away to some kinder and softer Climate, and never return till the Frosts are past, and the Winds are laid at home." The Netherlands was the first European country to stop persecuting people suspected of witchcraft—what was probably the last witch trial there in 1610 ended in acquittal. Foreign students came to Dutch universities, and philosophers—like Descartes—found the atmosphere propitious for original thought. Germans came to join the Dutch East India Company, and

Human musculature, drawn from direct observation, for Andreas Vesalius' monumental work on anatomy, De humani corporis fabrica, *1543*

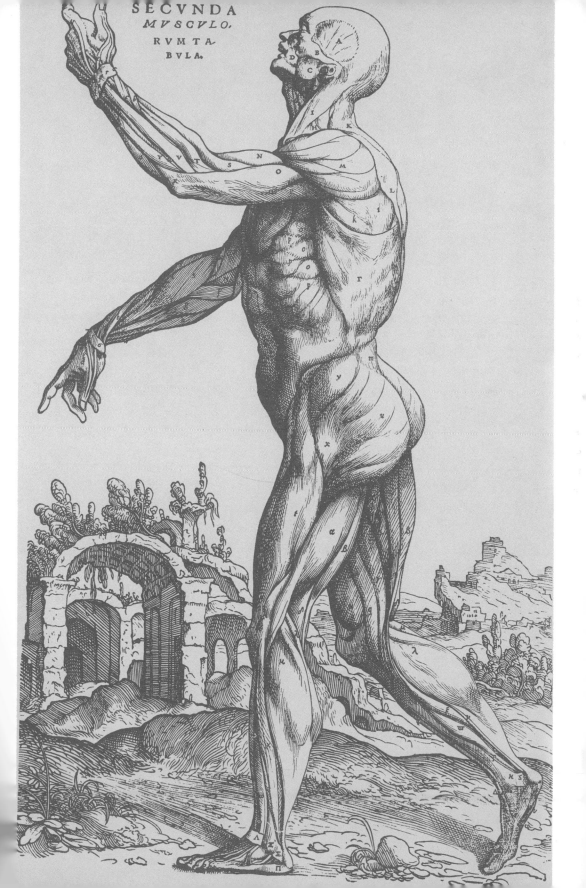

Jacob Poppen, who arrived penniless from Holstein, became a burgomaster of Amsterdam and died in 1624 a millionaire. English sailors
served in the Dutch fleets. For twelve years the Pilgrim fathers found
a friendly refuge in Leiden—"a fair and beauteous city of a sweet
situation," according to William Bradford, one of their leaders. William Brewster taught at the university and published Puritan books
which annoyed King James when they were brought into England.

The Dutch were born with one foot in the sea. Many of them lived
below sea level, and they grew up with the thought and fear of it, and
were intent on mastering it. Their large fishing fleet employed many
and taught them skills which they put to use on longer voyages. In the
course of forty years the Dutch crossed the oceans to found New
Amsterdam, Capetown, and Batavia, and to trade with the Japanese.
They left everywhere their own names—Rensselaer, Van Diemen, Tasman—and place names from their mother country—New Zealand,
Saint Martin, Cape Horn. Abel Tasman's first voyage around Australia
proved that it was an island continent. Willem Barents and Jan van
Heemskerk attempted to find a northeast passage to China, while
Netherlanders drained marshes in Russia. Dutch was the seventeenth
century's marine language in the Baltic; an inaugural lecture at Turku
University in Finland was delivered in Dutch; and in the North Sea
and English Channel, more sailors spoke Dutch than English. Many
Dutch terms were imbedded in the vocabulary of English sailors at this
time, and are still in use. Dutch ships carried most of the freight be-
tween England and Germany, and between England and France, and
even a good deal of coastal goods from one English port to another.
The sails of English ships were made from Dutch cloth. Such men as
Adriaen Block, who was shipwrecked on the wooded shores of Man-
hattan and built a new ship there, obtained a fearless reputation for
Dutch sea captains. Of one master it was said that "he would sail into
hell and trade with the devil were it not that his sails would catch fire."
A Chinese writer warned about the unscrupulous Dutch mariners: "If
meeting them at sea, one is certain to be robbed." They taught naviga-
tion to the Barbary pirates. Many "Moorish" pirates, in fact, were
Dutchmen. Under the name of Morate Reis lurked Jan Janszen of
Haarlem. Soliman Reis was the pseudonym of one Veenboer, killed
attacking a Christian ship in 1620. Dutch slave ships often sailed the

infamous Middle Passage between Guinea and Curaçao, rivaling the
Portuguese in their volume of human cargo. However, although the
Dutch were often brutes abroad, they kept the reputation of being
civilized at home; slaves were free once they touched Dutch soil.

On the Dutch command of sea depended much of their great seventeenth-century prosperity. Other factors were hard work, the pressure
of population, and the disorganization of rival nations. Foreigners
noted another Dutch characteristic that made for success: their pru-
dence. Sir William Temple thought, "their common riches lie in every
man's spending less than he has coming in." He added, "They buy in-
finitely but it is to sell again, either upon improvement of the com-
modity, or at a better market. They are the great masters of the Indian
spices, and of the Persian silks, but wear plain woollen, and feed upon
their own fish and roots." As today's Dutch export butter and eat mar-
garine, so then, Sir William noted, "they sell the finest of their own
cloth to France, and buy coarse out of England for their own wear."

Families were frugal, and so was the state. The States General had
to pay off debts incurred during the war of liberation, and some thirteen
million florins were still owed in 1660. There was, for the time, a high
rate of taxation, which the Dutch apparently bore with good will since
it went into projects for the public good. At the same time there was
a generally low rate of bank loan interest, around 3 per cent, the wonder of other nations. It made for a flexible economy. Merchants had
convenient and highly secure accounts in the Amsterdam banks.

Since the Netherlands had so few raw materials of its own, the
Dutch transported goods, improved them, and re-exported them. Their
situation at the mouth of the Rijn and Maas gave them an unrivaled
place on European trade routes. Their merchant fleet, with 2,400 ships
in 1670, was the biggest in the world. The docks of Amsterdam were
busy night and day, and to see the Indies fleet arrive was a spectacle no
one ever forgot.

An English visitor to Amsterdam in 1619, James Howell, wrote
home that it was rare to encounter a beggar. Everyone worked; major
employers were granaries, timber mills, shipyards, sugar refineries,
and gunpowder factories. Tapestries were woven there, diamonds polished, and marble cut. Sails and ropes were made for ships, and salt
treated for fishing boats to lay down their catches. Hard work had

more to do with the tough, demanding natural environment, perhaps, than with Calvinism, whose principles some historians see as the whip driving the Dutch people to great achievements. The modern historian Bernard Vlekke puts the argument well: "The moral principles of Calvinism and the rigidity of its tenets may have helped to foster the qualities of self-reliance and of persistence in a given task so typical of the Netherlanders; perhaps also a feeling of superiority, of being God's elect and as such above the masses outside His grace. But Calvinism certainly was not a dominating factor in the development. . . . In the few decades in which the sudden upsurge occurred, the dogma of Calvin had no more than a meager hold on the spirit of the leading Netherlanders."

Amsterdam was backed by an urban conglomeration of thriving towns; Zaandam with its wind-powered sawmills, Haarlem with its breweries, Leiden producing textiles, Gouda making pikes and ropes, Delft with its pottery. It was a small area. Huizinga points out that "Dutch civilization in Rembrandt's day was concentrated in a region not much more than sixty miles square." But however small, it fostered a society in which all the elements of culture thrived. Education had a wide base for the time. Each town had its Latin school, like the one Rembrandt attended as a boy in Leiden. The three Rs were taught in a preparatory grade, and the classics followed. While the sons of professional and merchant classes went to the Latin schools, their sisters attended the fashionable French schools, run by Huguenot refugees. Common schools provided the rudiments of an elementary education for the less well-to-do. Sir Josiah Child, an English visitor, wrote, "A Dutchman, however inferior in class or station he may be, always takes care that his children learn to write a good hand and the art of counting." What a village school was like is suggested in Jan Steen's painting in the National Gallery of Scotland. Some children in the one-room establishment have colored picture alphabet books. One little girl has hanging from her waist a wooden board with writing on it. The "unstructured" nature of the place is perhaps indicated by the fact that several of the children are clearly up to some mischief, and one is fast asleep. There is a live parrot, and plants creeping in from outside. An edict of 1655 demonstrated some dissatisfaction with infant schools: teacher candidates from this date were required to be able to read

A cotton wall hanging from India depicts richly arrayed Dutch colonials enjoying the fruits of their labors amid the splendors of an Oriental court.

printed and manuscript writing, know hymns and be able to write.

At Leiden University students came from all over Europe, not only to attend the famous medical school, but to study theology, the classics, natural history, astronomy, Hebrew, and Arabic. The university's Botanic Garden, under the direction of Charles de Lécluse, known as Clusius, provided herbs, which were then the indispensable raw materials for drugs. In this atmosphere, superstition and the hocus-pocus of alchemy and astrology were pushed back by science, served by such illustrious men as Simon Stevin, Anton van Leeuwenhoek, Christian Huyghens, and Jan Swammerdam. There was nothing rarified about them: their ideas grew out of practical experience. Van Leeuwenhoek —born in Delft in 1632, the same year as his fellow townsman Jan Vermeer—was a bookkeeper by profession, by avocation a scientist. He ground and polished lenses of considerable magnifying power, and mounted them in single-lens microscopes. He was among the first to perfect such instruments for intelligent discovery, and thus to see microbes. He called them "little animacules." He was the first to describe human blood corpuscles. His discoveries of protozoa and bacteria in rain water brought him recognition in Holland from the statesman and poet Constantijn Huyghens, and from the Royal Society of England, which made him a Fellow. He wrote to the secretary of the Society, after examining a phial of lake water: "And the motion of most of these animacules in the water was so swift, and so various, upwards, downwards, and round about, that 'twas wonderful to see. . . ."

In the discovery of the minute world that had been existing under the noses of men, an equally perspicacious contemporary was the anatomist Jan Swammerdam, who studied insect life. Most people then thought insects were spontaneously generated from mud and manure. Swammerdam, following the course of insect life, showed that "just as all vegetation evolves from a perceptible and fertile seed, even so all other creatures and animals spring from a seed or egg." He found that snails were hermaphrodites. He described the division of work arranged by bees in a hive. And his work on the May fly is full of wonder: "Nothing seems to me more remarkable than that it does not try to postpone the time of its metamorphosis. It casts off as soon as it can the shape of a creeping and swimming worm to assume the figure of a flying creature." From which fact Swammerdam, who was highly religious, drew the moral—"This teaches man that he should quickly and readily leave the wet and cold waters of this muddy vale and raise himself on the wings of hope and love, which are the two arms of faith, into the air of divine affections."

Unlike Swammerdam, Constantijn Huyghens' son Christian was a rationalist, and no great patriot. He said, "The world is my country, to promote science my religion." This made him a rather lonely figure in that committed age. But he was celebrated throughout Europe by the age of thirty. Louis XIV gave him a pension and an apartment. He invented the pendulum clock, worked out a theory of light, and studied the composition of Saturn's ring (now known to be four rings).

Telescopes were in those days invaluable at sea, and the art of making lenses a splendid apprenticeship in applied science. Huyghens, Swammerdam, and Leeuwenhoek all made and looked through lenses. Hermann Boerhaave, the great medical researcher at Leiden, born the year before Rembrandt's death, translated into Latin a treatise on glass polishing by Huyghens. Baruch Spinoza made lenses for a living while pondering the infinity of God through the powerful lens of his mind.

Born in Amsterdam of Portuguese-Jewish refugee parents, Spinoza horrified the orthodox rabbis with his "heretical" thought. After being excommunicated from the synagogue, he left Amsterdam for the village of Rijnsburg, near Leiden. The Calvinist ministers thought him an atheist. The synod of South Holland referred to his *Tractatus theologico-politicus* (Treatise on religious and political philosophy) as a "dirty and truly blasphemous book." Spinoza considered the universe an organic whole, in which God was expressed, and the Bible a historical document about institutions intended only for the ancient Jews. But he saw the advantages of contemporary Holland. "We have the rare felicity of living in a state where entire freedom of opinion prevails, where all may worship God in their own fashion, and where nothing is held sweeter, nothing more precious than such liberty."

A philosopher who exercised much influence on the Dutch, including Spinoza, was René Descartes, who lived in Holland for thirty years. He noted the amenities and the anonymity of urban life there, then as now, "being among the crowd of a great and energetic people, who are more concerned with their own affairs than curious about other people's, yet lack none of the conveniences to be found in the most populous towns." In Amsterdam he was able to live "as solitary and as undisturbed as in the farthest deserts. . . . Everyone is so preoccupied with his own gain that I could live there all my life without ever being seen by a soul." Descartes' *Discourse on Method* (1637) was published by Jean Le Maire of Leiden (the author received two hundred copies in payment), and the Calvinist synod of South Holland protested against the teaching of his philosophy at Leiden University.

Two particularly practical great men of that age were Simon Stevin and Jan Adriaanszoon, later called Leeghwater. Stevin was a well-rounded genius—an astronomer, a mathematician, and an engineer. He wrote a navigational handbook for determining one's position at sea. His manual of bookkeeping was helpful in sorting out French national finances. He wrote about music, civics, and the use of the Dutch language—for which he was well qualified, since he spurned Latin and wrote all his works in his native tongue. Stevin taught the arts of fortification at Prince Maurice's military academy, improved the cannon, and —among other things—invented a sleigh driven by sail.

Sails also drove the windmills, which helped drain Holland. This was the ambition of Leeghwater—meaning "rid water." He promoted the draining of the 18,000-acre Beemstermeer—a feat accomplished with the aid of forty windmills between 1608 and 1612. This encouraged the draining of other lakes and led Leeghwater to propose his grandest scheme—to drain the Haarlemmermeer. This inland sea had doubled in size since 1500. Its banks were constantly washing away and its choppy waters often made for dangerous voyages between Leiden and Amsterdam. Leeghwater claimed that the waters of the Haarlemmermeer covered splendidly fertile soil, but his project was buried in argument. For one thing, Leiden got its drinking water from the lake. Furthermore, the cost of the project, though small per acre, seemed vast in sum. Opponents said five hundred windmills would be needed. Thus it was not until 1836, some two hundred years later, that work was started, after an immense flood had threatened Amsterdam, Haarlem, and Leiden. By then, there were pumps driven by steam engines to help drain the lake. The ground proved to be tremendously fertile, as Leeghwater had claimed.

In the meantime, windmills turned all over the below-sea-level Netherlands. The mill was a brilliant method of harnessing natural

Seventeenth-century Dutchmen toasted their new-found prosperity with lavishly wrought silver cups, like this inverted goblet with windmill stem.

forces, the power of the wind transmitted through canvas, wood, and stone into productive energy. In the fifteenth century the invention of the rotating cap enabled the sails to be pointed directly into the wind without pivoting the entire mill. The wooden gears were harnessed to machinery which not only "milled" grain but drove circular saws. Windmills on the canals in reclamation works pumped water by means of a scoop wheel from the drowned land into channels and thence into rivers and the sea; and as the water level sank, new canals were dug, and new windmills built to pump the remaining water away. In Zaandam by 1700 some six hundred sawmills, powered by the wind, formed a sizable industrial area. Other mills made paper, vegetable oil, and gunpowder. Rembrandt's father was a miller in Leiden. And long before they were made clichés on tiles, plates, and souvenirware, the mills became landmarks and message carriers, signaling births, marriages, and deaths; the particular event indicated by a certain arrangement of the sails, visible from afar.

Dutch seamen brought back from distant voyages accounts of exotic objects and fantastic places. Illustrated travel journals were popular reading. It was said that on an Arctic island Dutch sailors discovered four hundred wooden statues buried in the ice. From Mauritius a Dutch ship brought back a strange, plump, flightless bird called the Dodo, which would shortly be extinct, though not before several artists, including Roelant Savery, had painted its portrait. The Dutch taste for the exotic was given fullest expression in the tulip madness, which seized the Netherlands in the 1630s. The tulip had been found by the Crusaders along the roadsides of Asia Minor. It was cultivated in Turkish monasteries, and coveted by sultans and rich merchants. From Turkey the flower came to Austria in 1554. The Hapsburg court gardener, a Dutchman, introduced the tulip to Holland, and affection for the flower soon spread to, and was heightened by, the French court of Louis XIII. In Holland the bulbs grew well in the coarse sandy soil behind the coastal dunes. Varieties of tulips could be produced in small gardens. Virus diseases brought about vivid, bizarre coloring effects, which made the tulip even more attractive. Soon half the population seemed to be tulip-crazy.

The infatuation seized people of all classes and incomes. Painters, like Judith Leyster, pupil of Frans Hals, were commissioned to paint

albums of tulip portraits. In Haarlem the guild of weavers speculated
in tulip bulbs as prices rose and rare varieties sold for fantastic sums.
In 1637, the peak year of tulip mania, ten million guilders changed
hands in one town alone in tulip transactions. Some bulbs were traded
several times in one day. At Hoorn three rare bulbs were enough to
buy a house. Thieves stole tulip bulbs instead of cash, and citizens
guarded their plots with alarm bells and wire. One brewer offered his
brewery in exchange for a single bulb. The bubble burst in February,
1637. Many were ruined, left holding bulbs or debts for bulbs that they
now could not sell. The bankrupts included the painter Jan van Goyen.
Those who had kept their heads referred to the tulip-crazy as "hooded
ones"—an allusion to the hoods worn by madmen.

Perhaps the tulip madness had offered some relief from the long
hours of hard work which was the common lot. Women and children
worked too—indeed, many industries hired them because they could
be paid less. Long vacations were not known, and numerous Catholic
holidays had been abolished by the Reformation. Many worked a seven-
day week and in some poor families children were sent out to forage
in the streets after they returned home from work.

Yet a rough-and-ready egalitarianism prevailed. There was no lower-
class servility. Parival, the French professor at Leiden, said he had
never seen such treatment of servants elsewhere—he was quite upset
by the insolence of Dutch maids. The state placed a heavy tax on employers of male servants, which reduced their numbers even in the
houses of the great. No physical punishment of servants was allowed
—a regulation which amazed foreign visitors. Moreover, Admiral de
Ruyter's wife could be seen in the Amsterdam streets, alone and on
foot, with her shopping basket over her arm. She hung out her own
washing, and the day after her husband's death was unable to receive
a visit from the prince of Orange because she had slipped and hurt herself putting out the laundry.

The drink of the great majority was beer—drunk at every meal and
at taverns in between. "The qualities in their air may incline them to
drinking," Temple wrote. "It may be necessary to thaw and move the
frozen and inactive spirits of the brain." Women drank as much as
men, and at celebrations toast followed toast, and the host felt insulted
if the guests were not as drunk as himself. In Haarlem in 1600, the

Admiral van der Eijck

1643

annual consumption of beer was reckoned to be five and a half *million* gallons—enough to provide every man, woman, and child with about three quarters of a gallon a day.

It was also a century in which tobacco and tea became fashionable; Clusius at Leiden grew the newfangled potato as an ornamental vegetable; and everyone began to take snuff—everyone, that is, except the Anabaptists. Not all the old feasts had been stamped out by the Calvinists—Twelfth Night went on being celebrated with pageants of the Three Kings. At Noordwijk on that day a procession of children went from door to door collecting cheese, bread, and money. On Martinmas, the eleventh of November, a sort of Thanksgiving was held with roast goose and new wine, bonfires and singing. On Saint Nicholas' Day the children got presents as they had done (and still do) since the thirteenth century. There were also, as in medieval times, kermises—week-long local fairs where goods were bought and sold and the people of a community enjoyed themselves. The kermis was opened by a parade and an archery competition. Bakers sold their special kermis cakes. Clowns and acrobats performed, people sang and danced, and the dancing and drinking often ended in brawling and fighting.

The kermises provided one occasion for young people to get together in liberated conditions. In The Hague, a Reformed pastor named Eleazar Lotius claimed that some people went to church solely for amorous rendezvous. But they did not need to go to that extreme if they lived in such places as the island of Texel, where on the night of April 30 the young men and women danced round bonfires; nor for that matter, if they lived in many country villages where "trial" marriages became the real thing if the girl got pregnant. Church and State condemned funeral feasts, but they remained popular, especially in the most northerly provinces. All who had known a man during his lifetime would turn up at these ceremonies after the funeral to drink a toast to the departed, and the wake was often boisterous indeed. Nevertheless, many foreign visitors took home from Holland doubts about the Dutch capacity for passionate emotions. The natives struck Sir William Temple as too "temperate." The Frenchman René Le Pays complained that a Dutchwoman in the midst of making love was liable to start eating an apple or breaking nuts with her teeth.

In the paintings that tell us so much about the Netherlands at this

An illustration from Judith Leyster's tulip album, produced in 1643

time the favorite winter sport is ice skating. During cold weather the water country became a land of ice. In Hendrik Avercamp's paintings women push children across the ice in sleighs that are wooden boxes or chairs on runners. As fishermen cut numerous holes in the ice, some skaters strapped wooden poles to their shoulders to hold them up if they fell in. Men played a game called *kolf,* from which golf is said to have come—though in the paintings it also looks like an ancestor of ice hockey. (Then as now children in all seasons played such games as I spy, hunt the slipper, prisoner's base, conkers, marbles, blindman's buff, and leapfrog.)

In wintertime skating on the canals was also a good way of getting around the country. You could skate from Leiden to Amsterdam in an hour and a quarter. Alternatively, stagecoaches ran most of the year, taking forty-two hours, for example, between Groningen and Amsterdam—but prices were high and discomfort considerable. Since the fifteenth century a public water transport system had spread, and at this point embraced nearly the whole country. Canals in that watery landscape were a quarter of the cost of roads. The *trekschuit,* a long, horse-drawn barge, carried some fifty passengers. In the cabin of the barge they could sleep, eat, gossip, or sing. (Songbooks were kept on board for those who wanted to exercise their voices.) Though slower than stagecoaches, the canalboats were frequent and reliable. On some lines there was even a night service.

John Evelyn, an eminent English visitor in the seventeenth century, noticed the remarkable popularity of paintings. Works of art were on sale at markets and fairs. They were to be found in offices and homes, in town halls, almshouses, and the clubrooms of militia companies. The art of painting was pursued by many amateurs and professionals. People wanted to hang on their walls country scenes, seascapes, still lifes, and portraits. And to fulfill this need, this tiny part of the world's surface produced several generations of great painters. "They were born everywhere at once," wrote the nineteenth-century French critic Eugène Fromentin—"at Amsterdam, at Dordrecht, at Leiden, Delft, Utrecht, Rotterdam, Enkhuizen, Haarlem." Hals was born in Antwerp around 1583 and moved to Haarlem. There followed Jan van Goyen, born 1596; Rembrandt, 1606; Adriaen van Ostade, 1610; Terborch, 1617; Albert Cuyp, 1620; Paul Potter, 1625; Jan Steen, 1626; Gabriel Metsu,

A Dutch gentleman purchases a bottle of French wine—or possibly stronger spirits like Holland gin—at a well-stocked apothecary shop.

1629; Jacob van Ruisdael, 1630; Jan Vermeer, 1632—not to mention Pieter de Hooch, Meindert Hobbema, Jan van de Cappelle, Hercules Seghers, Pieter Janszoon Saenredam, Nicolaes Maes, Nicolaes Berchem, Willem van Aelst, and so many others.

These painters inherited a tradition of professional craftsmanship. Painting was work to which one was apprenticed and in which one spent years learning from, and assisting, a master in his studio. An apprentice had to copy antique works and do the groundwork on paintings which the master would finish, touch up, and sell as his own. Paintings were mostly small, to fit on the walls of the average house. Fortunately, not too many Dutch artists made the fashionable trip to Italy, or were unduly affected by academic considerations. When there were artistic conventions to be fulfilled, such as the group portrait, these proved to be forms within which Hals and Rembrandt immortalized individuals and the age they lived in.

Sincerity, clarity, concern—these are words that come to mind as one looks at the paintings of the age. In this art, Fromentin wrote, "we feel a loftiness and a goodness of heart, an affection for the true, a love for the real, that give their works a value the things do not seem to possess." The Church and the aristocracy were no longer great patrons. The demand of the merchant class was rather for painting that was simple, commonplace, and everyday, and perhaps it is not astonishing that this demand called into being a school of painters whose work was unique—the close and loving examination of the commonplace being, more often than not, a good recipe for masterpieces. The Dutch painters presented landscapes now not just as background but as arrangements of trees and buildings, as descriptions of light and weather —as testimony to the beauty they saw in nature and man's reordering of it. This art did not always appeal to foreign taste. A Frenchman visiting Delft in 1663 thought a painting by Vermeer overvalued at six hundred guilders because it had but one figure in it.

Vermeer was a tavern proprietor, art dealer, and master painter. He recognized the quality of street life, of ordinary houses and passageways and the activity that went on in them. His "View of Delft" achieves—with what effort, painstaking experience, and technique!— a magical spontaneity. It seizes for all time a Dutch day of bright sunshine between showers, with the wind blowing fresh from the southwest. And when he moves indoors, Vermeer continues to use the Dutch light. It illuminates conversations and silences, coming in through doors and windows on a girl playing the virginal or reading a letter or dozing at a table covered with a bright carpet. We are shown the tiles on the floor, brass studs that hold the leather upholstery on the chairs, maps of Europe hanging on the walls.

The life reflected in these paintings is assured, unhurried, full of rich content—though Vermeer himself, like Hals and Rembrandt, was probably often in debt. After his father's death, Vermeer took over the family tavern and art dealership, but with a wife and eleven children to keep his expenses were large. From what little we know of him he painted slowly. His pictures were fairly high-priced for the time, but he painted few. His recognized skills as an artist in Delft did not prevent him from being insolvent when he died in 1675 at the age of forty-four. Vermeer's work was the highest expression of Dutch life in the art of his time. Rembrandt, on the other hand, though very much a Dutchman, transcends any regional or epochal qualifications. He painted Dutch burghers and their wives, he drew small farmhouses and river scenes. But where other Dutch artists might be stuck in one specialty or other, Rembrandt painted and drew in all and every one, and created several original genres of his own. He painted Jewish rabbis, Mennonite preachers, old women, babies, Oriental potentates, Biblical scenes, and theatrical compositions of himself and his wife or of militia companies going on watch. He painted anatomy lessons and group portraits, such as "The Syndics of the Cloth Drapers Guild," that fit into recognized categories; but he painted them in ways that no one else would have dreamed of. His "Conspiracy of Julius Civilis" is a group portrait depicting a scene from Roman-Gallic history—and the old warrior not at all the suitably aristocratic rebel that those who commissioned it for the new Amsterdam town hall would have liked to see. Rembrandt's etchings and drawings, freed from any temptation toward the extravagant and monumental by the very nature of the media involved, are often superbly simple and immensely moving. As for the self-portraits painted over the years, they remain the greatest testimony in paint any man has ever made of his own presence, his own life.

Rembrandt for all this had a typically Dutch weakness for things. He collected all sorts of objects, clothes, armor, and paintings by other

OVERLEAF: *Ice skaters on the Vijver, an artificial lake in The Hague, exhibit their prowess as Prince Maurice of Orange-Nassau and his party watch.*

artists. He painted himself and his wife Saskia rollicking about in embarrassing finery—perhaps an escape from the prevailing ethos of thrift and sobriety. He wanted a bigger and better house. For a while he earned a great income (1,600 guilders for "The Night Watch," and 2,400 guilders in 1646 from the prince of Orange for a small "Adoration of the Shepherds"). But in time his work became more profound and less fashionable. Although he retained important customers, his impulsive spending and big debt on his house brought about a forced sale of his possessions. The inventory revealed the extent of his acquisitions: ancient busts of Roman emperors, shells and minerals, a lion's skin, items from the Far East and Turkey. Saskia died in 1642, and because of conditions in the bequest of her estate—income which Rembrandt needed—he never formally married Hendrickje Stoffels, with whom he lived from 1645 to her death in 1663; but Hendrickje and his son Titus got him out of trouble after he was declared insolvent by forming a business partnership. Rembrandt promised to hand over to them as dealers all his work, in return for their support.

In 1654 Hendrickje gave birth to a daughter, Cornelia. While pregnant she had been called before the Reformed Church authorities and criticized for living with Rembrandt in an unmarried state. But she went on living with him. Tolerance in Dutch society then was ambiguous. The police levied a heavy, unofficial tax on Catholics. Calvinist synods complained frequently about the recurrence of Catholic worship in secret. The Reformed Church proclaimed in its confession of faith: "The office of the magistracy is to prevent and to eradicate all idolatry and false religion and to destroy the kingdom of Anti-Christ." But many families remained Catholic, and many people became converts. Such Catholics as the poet and playwright Joost van den Vondel could still be Dutch patriots. Catholics were excluded from public office, but most of them were allowed to live and worship quietly.

Political intolerance bit more deeply. One notable victim was a non-Catholic but a dissenter from the Calvinist orthodoxy, Hugo Grotius. Grotius (1583–1645) is considered by many Dutch historians to be the greatest scholar and man of letters the Netherlands has produced. A writer on law, on war and peace, he was driven from the country in 1619, returned once, but had to flee again because he was too closely allied with a group of oligarchs then out of power. Condemned to life

imprisonment, he escaped in a trunk. He went to live in Paris as Sweden's ambassador to the French court and—ahead of his time—wrote
about unjust wars and the freedom of the seas.

Although there was sufficient opportunity in the Netherlands to
make it the wonder of other countries in that doctrinaire, authoritarian
age, it was no democracy. Grotius himself believed that the leading men
of a community should control it—offering the title of leader to the
prince, but not letting either him or the masses take control. (Grotius
found in Tacitus' account of the revolt of the Batavian Julius Civilis
and his "leading men" a prototype of the provincial States, and therefore dated this institution back to the Germanic tribes.) Seventeenth-
century Holland was ruled by a small group of patricians, the upper
crust of the some-ten-thousand-strong bourgeoisie. These gentlemen,
holding the effective political power, ran a partly medieval, highly de-
centralized government while in other countries royal absolutism and
administrative centralization was in fashion. The patricians were often
called "regents," because they also presided as regents or trustees over
charitable foundations. They called themselves *Herren,* or Lordships,
so that they would not be confused with ordinary burghers. This caste
of ruling families—which produced such leaders as Johan van Oldenbarneveldt and Jan De Witt—was self-perpetuating. The members of
town councils decided who would fill council vacancies, and elected
new burgomasters and jurors. But again, compared with the governments of other countries at the time, the system had good points. Although the regents were not particularly interested in liberty, they were
opposed to the more tyrannical aspects of Calvinist theocracy, and they
were concerned to see that no one pressure group dominated affairs.
There was less corruption in the Netherlands than in most other European administrations. Few great landowners threw their weight and
influence around. (The small nobility, according to Paul Zumthor,
"lived like exiles in the heart of a nation of traders and merchants.")
Moreover, the style of the regents had effects up and down the social
scale. The princes of Orange with few exceptions led fairly simple
lives, without grand establishments or ornate palaces. The lesser bourgeoisie adopted the formal, earnest manner of the regents, although—
removed from political responsibility—they were almost totally absorbed in commercial activity.

124   It was, however, a constrained form of government, and pressure built up on several occasions to boiling and indeed exploding points. There were seven provincial States, which represented provincial interests. It was hard to get unanimous agreement in the national States General, in which each province had one vote and veto power. Moreover, internal loyalties ran in two main currents. First, there were those who wanted a country united on a federal basis, under the firm leadership of the stadholders provided by the House of Orange. Secondly, there were those who believed in states' rights and the power of provincial leaders or pensionaries, and in particular Hollanders who believed in the hegemony of the province of Holland—which provided most of the confederation's funds and most of the energy. The basic quarrel was colored by religious dissension. The Calvinists were split into two factions on the subject of predestination. A professor at Leiden called Franciscus Gomarus upheld the dogma while another Leiden professor, Jacobus Arminius, rejected it. The States of Holland under Oldenbarneveldt supported the more liberal, Arminian view. Prince Maurice of Orange led the Gomarist and therefore anti-Holland party —he had nontheological motives as well, since he was annoyed by the military calm which the oligarchs of Holland, under Oldenbarneveldt, maintained by preserving the truce with Spain. Maurice received the support of the States General, except for the delegation from Utrecht and Holland. He had Oldenbarneveldt and other leaders arrested. Oldenbarneveldt had antagonized too many Orangists; and though he was, in the words of the register of the States of Holland, "a man of great activity, business, memory and wisdom, yes extraordinary in every respect," he paid the price of unpopularity on the wider, national scale. On May 13, 1619, after a mock trial, the seventy-year-old grand pensionary was beheaded. He said on the scaffold: "Do not believe that I am a traitor to my country."

This reduced for the moment the power of Holland, and the prince of Orange, backed by the States General, now wielded supreme authority; but by mid-century the wheel would turn full circle. A generation after Oldenbarneveldt's execution, Holland reappeared as the leader of a provincial coalition. Its will and money held the republic together. This time the first man of the oligarchy was Jan De Witt. Sir William Temple called him "the perfect Hollander." De Witt came

Created in 1670, Vermeer's late masterpiece, "The Art of Painting," features a self-portrait of the artist in his softly illuminated, well-appointed studio.

from a family of Dordrecht merchants, studied law at Leiden, went on a European Grand Tour, practiced law in The Hague, and wrote both poetry and a treatise on conical sections which one historian has called "the first textbook of analytical geometry."

De Witt was twenty-eight when he rose from pensionary or chief magistrate of Dordrecht to the post of Grand Pensionary of Holland, a combination of legal adviser and administrator. For nearly three decades, until 1672, he maintained the authority of the Dutch oligarchy in its traditional opposition to the House of Orange. (In this he had the noble example of his father who had been imprisoned by William II for trying to thwart the prince's wartime pro-French policy.) Thus the long struggle went on between the states' rights regents and the Orangists, who had the support of the masses, the army, and much of the navy, and favored a strong central government under the Nassau dynasty. De Witt managed to abolish the office of commander in chief, hitherto held by the stadholder, the prince of Orange. He not only directed the republic's foreign policy but became its *de facto* head. He was honest, worked hard, and in his haughty way steered the country ably through a turbulent era. He strengthened the United Provinces' navy. On one occasion, when the fleet lay in an exposed anchorage, with a storm rising and the naval commanders disagreeing with one another, De Witt himself led the ships safely out to sea. He commanded missions to other provinces in attempts to help them solve their domestic difficulties. He was a wizard at drawing unanimous agreements from the disputatious States Assemblies, to which town delegations came with their own, highly self-interested points of view.

But none of this made him popular. De Witt believed that he knew best. He thought of himself as "a wise and stern father who, if he should yield to the will and inclinations of his children, would be likely to do them serious harm." This attitude of benevolent superiority was characteristic of the Dutch patrician class. Sometimes referred to as "the regent's mentality," it hung on for several centuries, copied by the burghers, in some ways stultifying the culture of the Netherlands, and increasingly manifested in a form of snobbish complacency. Yet there was no pretension in De Witt's way of life. He usually walked, and saved his carriage for official occasions. His household was run on customary Dutch bourgeois lines, and though he had several servants at the expense of the state he did many of his own chores. Foreign visitors were astonished at this austerity; some found it slightly arrogant.

During the years of De Witt's administration the two Dutch empires, East and West, experienced different fortunes. The empire in the Americas was not long-lasting. The Amsterdam merchants were more interested in trade and privateering than in settlement. For a while it seemed that the Dutch flag was destined to fly over a great Brazilian colony, part of the Caribbean, and North American estates stretching along the Hudson, Mohawk, and Connecticut rivers; but by 1670 all that remained were a few Caribbean islands, part of Guiana, and—on the other side of the Atlantic—some trading posts in West Africa. Brazil and New Amsterdam were gone.

The West India Company had worked on the faulty assumption that it could combine empire building with plundering the Spanish. Furthermore, the Dutch attacked the Portuguese, thus alienating their logical allies against Spain. The Dutch soon lost their monopoly of the slave trade as the British muscled their way in on the profitable business. Mistakes were also made in North America: the fur trade was badly run, immigration was not properly encouraged, and the governors, chosen through nepotism, ruled with a heavy hand. The English crowded into North America and soon occupied the lands on the Connecticut River. New Amsterdam's inhabitants spoke some eighteen different languages (according to the Jesuit Father Isaac Jogues who was there in 1634), and the religious life was diversified by Lutherans and Quakers, alongside the original Walloons and Dutch Reformed settlers. Even so, though a shortage of energetic pioneers persisted and New Amsterdam was lost to the English during one of the Anglo-Dutch wars in the second half of the century, Dutch influence remained strongly felt in North America in business, language, and systems of land tenure. The Holland Land Company speculated in wide tracts of Pennsylvania and New York in 1795; an American of Dutch blood dug the Erie Canal; and the early Roosevelts ran a steamboat service from Pittsburgh to Natchez.

The Dutch seventeenth-century emigrants preferred to settle in places close to home, where there were no Indian raiding parties to be braved or long ocean journeys to be suffered in getting there. Many of those who left the Netherlands in large numbers in those years moved to Holstein. German princes whose states had been devastated in the Thirty Years' War sought colonists from Friesland and Zeeland. Other Dutchmen went to England as engineers, to drain the Fens and build harbors.

Despite the Dutch nation's lack of success in the New World, the mercantile empire in Asia and the East Indies flourished. The East India Company gained a monopoly of Asiatic textiles through its control of southern Indian ports. The seas of that region were dominated by the Dutch. The company suffered a setback when it lost Formosa (Taiwan), base for the China trade, but otherwise it prospered, governing its territories firmly if rigidly, from its headquarters at Batavia. Although company profits came first, the company sponsored research in areas that might contribute to the economic well-being of its enterprise. It aided studies directed at reducing disease on the long sea voyage to the East; research into Eastern religion, botany, and languages was not discouraged; schools for native children were opened in Batavia, and Christianity took a back seat when the support was needed of native princes, upholders of Islam—though here and there some natives already converted to Catholicism by Portuguese Jesuits were further converted to Calvinism. The company directors paid for the translation of the Bible into Malay.

Throughout this period of boisterous Dutch expansion, problems with England mounted. On the English side existed a feeling that the Dutch were upstarts, helped into being by Elizabeth and Leicester. To the English, Dutch commercial and naval success was often galling. On Amboina, in the Moluccas, some English traders were executed by the Dutch in 1623 on a charge of conspiracy. The bitter memory of this event stayed with the English for at least half a century. (John Dryden based a play on the incident and Andrew Marvell wrote a scathing poem about the Dutch, "The Character of Holland.") In 1626 the States General took away from the British ambassador the membership in the Council of State that had been granted in exchange for Elizabeth's military aid. On top of this, in 1639 came the greatest blow to English pride. A Spanish fleet, battered by Dutch ships under Admiral Maarten Tromp, had taken refuge in the Downs, an anchorage on the English coast near Dover. Tromp challenged the Spanish to come out and fight; they refused, and he sailed in—despite the presence of an English squadron. He destroyed most of the Spanish fleet while it was in English waters.

The long truce with Spain had finally ended, but war this time did not last long. Despite Tromp's naval victories and Prince Frederick Henry's military success in regaining much of North Brabant and Limburg, most of the Dutch wanted peace. And it was finally, conclusively made in the Peace of Westphalia, signed at Münster in 1648: the last of the Spanish yoke thrown off by the northern provinces; the Hapsburg connection completely severed. The southern Netherlands had reverted to Spain on the death of Archduke Albert in 1621. The Archduchess Isabella remained as the king's representative until her death in 1633. France coveted the region, but the Dutch, by concluding a separate peace with Spain, ensured that the southern provinces remained as a buffer zone between them and all-powerful France.

During the second half of the century relations between France, England, and Holland had little consistency. Fear of the French occasionally brought the two maritime powers together, so much so that in 1649 there were plans for a political union between the two countries. But though Holland and England were then very much alike, and had great influence on each other (it was easier to get from London to Amsterdam than from London to many English provincial cities), they were also rivals for the same goals. At sea, the Dutch—with the biggest merchant fleet—championed free trade and unrestricted navigation. The English attempted to undercut the Dutch lead by passing protectionist measures, in particular the Navigation Acts which insisted that foreign goods imported into England be carried either in English ships or ships from the country in which the goods originated. The English wanted the Dutch to salute their flag in English waters and demanded the right to stop and search neutral vessels, including Dutch vessels, for contraband. Furthermore, rival colonial interests in West Africa and North America provided plenty of points for friction. The result was that three wars between England and the United Provinces took place while De Witt was grand pensionary; the first, from 1652 to 1654; the second, 1664 to 1667; the third, 1672 to 1678.

Even at war, restraining, contradictory forces appeared. During the Protectorate in England, Cromwell realized that defeating Protestant Holland could only aid England's archenemy, Catholic France. Royal

relations provided additional entanglements. The exiled Stuarts took refuge on Dutch soil. (During their continental wanderings, the court of Charles II also stayed in Bruges and in Brussels where they left many debts). When Charles II was restored to the English throne in 1660, the Dutch presented him with a yacht—giving the Dutch sport of small boat sailing an overseas hold too. Charles' sister, Mary, was married to William II of Nassau, and Charles' nephew, William III, married his own cousin, James II's daughter, which made William a suitable person to share the British throne when James was forced out.

At sea, supremacy passed back and forth. During the first conflict, the English generals-at-sea Black and Monck, together with Admirals Penn and Lawson, decisively whipped the Dutch. In the second war the Dutch began badly. Jacob van Wassenaer van Obdam, the Dutch commander in chief, had little naval skill, and in an encounter with the English his flagship *Eendracht* blew up. Then, wrote Admiral Tromp, "The fleet got into such a confusion that they all ran away from the enemy before the wind, and through that some ships fell afoul of each other [and were] taken or burned by the English." But Tromp and his

colleague, Admiral Johan Evertsen, got the larger part of the Dutch fleet safely to port. Admiral Michel de Ruyter proceeded to build up a navy, turning merchant skippers and freebooters into disciplined naval commanders. The Dutch therefore did better in the Four Days' Battle of 1660 and in 1667 carried out a brilliant attack on the Medway estuary, burning and carrying off English ships, including the flagship, the *Royal Charles,* and causing great panic in London. Besides all this, the wars achieved little beyond the financial exhaustion of the participants and the crippling and impoverishment of thousands of seamen. But they provided splendid opportunities for Dutch maritime painters. Jan van de Cappelle, Hendrick Vroom, Hendrick Dubbels, Jan Porcellis, and Abraham Storck established a great seascape tradition, within which the Van de Velde family excelled with portraits of ships and engagements, calms and storms. Admiral de Ruyter ordered one skipper, Govert Pieterse, to take Willem van de Velde the Elder in his sloop for close-up studies of the fleet in action.

During the second Anglo-Dutch war the French occupied part of the southern Netherlands, and though (by the Treaty of Aix-la-

Whether of men or women, young or old, Rembrandt's portraits invariably reflect their maker's mastery of the art of subtle characterization.

Chapelle) Louis XIV agreed to certain withdrawals, he maintained troops in some frontier towns. For the next forty years France continued to seek what she considered to be her "natural" frontiers in the Spanish Netherlands. Similar aggressive tendencies in the north were inhibited by the United Provinces' desire to keep the south as a buffer zone and to keep Antwerp in its closed, noncompetitive position. In the south out of the spotlight, it seemed to be mostly the Church that thrived: most especially the Jesuits flourished, founding schools and convents, and the public turned to penitence and mysticism under the renewed influence of Spain. The boom in religion had practical effects. Religious art works were once again in great demand to fill the churches cleaned out by the Calvinists and iconoclasts. Moreover, Antwerp still had powerful traditions and old established wealth. It was the home of Van Dyck and Rubens, whose work was in many ways dissimilar to that going on in the north. Van Dyck painted with a cool, elegant distinction (which the Stuarts liked); Rubens robustly embodied the lush, extrovert sensations we now think of as "baroque." Pieter Geyl sees in Rubens' work evidence of the fervent, though externalized, religious life of the Counter Reformation.

Rubens was born in Westphalia in 1577. His Flemish father had been in trouble because of Calvinist sympathies and was detained there over an affair with William of Orange's wife, the princess of Saxony. Young Peter Paul Rubens came to Antwerp with his mother when he was ten, and there grew up in cosmopolitan court circles. He studied art with Antwerp masters and, after eight years in Italy, returned to the Flemish city. By the age of thirty-one he was well-known, deluged with commissions and pupils. His studio was a sort of painting factory, producing work of all categories. He influenced the architecture of churches and the craft of tapestry weaving in Brussels. He designed title pages for books turned out by the famed Plantin Press of Antwerp and of Leiden. He led the life of a great nobleman with a country mansion near Malines and an ornate town house in Antwerp. Grandiose arches and porticoes surrounded the courtyard in front of his studio—a room 45' by 35', with workshops above. Like his predecessor Jan van Eyck, Rubens was not only artist but diplomat; he carried on secret negotiations in Paris and London for the Infanta Isabella. And while abroad he acquired commissions to paint, for example, the panels in the Luxembourg Palace in Paris glorifying the career of France's queen Marie de Médicis and to decorate the ceiling of Charles I's banqueting house in Whitehall. He advised Charles on his collection of paintings and was rewarded with a knighthood. Eminently successful in his own time, a great draughtsman and colorist, Rubens is perhaps diminished only by comparison with his two Dutch contemporaries; for compared with Rembrandt his work often seems a trifle hearty, and compared with Hals, its heartiness seems a little hollow.

Rembrandt died in Amsterdam in 1669—a date that may serve to mark the closing of the Golden Age. Three years later Jan De Witt's position had become dangerously weak. The Orangist forces he had so much antagonized were encouraged by the sudden collapse of his foreign policy. Louis XIV had succeeded in detaching Charles II from the Triple Alliance formed by England, Sweden, and the United Provinces. When Charles and Louis attacked the Low Countries in the spring of 1672, popular pressure compelled the States of Holland to defy De Witt and appoint William, prince of Orange, commander of the army. William III was then twenty-one and had the job of opposing the best army of Europe with four thousand poorly trained men. But he also had the traditional Dutch advantage of the terrain; he withdrew his outnumbered forces behind the rivers, and, with the growing support of the people was appointed to the restored post of stadholder in both Holland and Zeeland.

De Witt handed in his resignation, but a month later he and his brother were savagely murdered in The Hague. Through his reorganization of Netherlands finances, his rebuilding of the Dutch navy, and his demonstration of the fact that the United Provinces was a European power, De Witt had created the conditions in which William was able to preserve Europe from Louis XIV's totalitarianism in the last quarter of the century. His death is still not easily digested by Dutch historians —"an act of perverted patriotism," Adriaan Barnouw calls it, while Bernard Vlekke writes that it was "the revenge of the middle class upon the fallen aristocracy." Like the death of Oldenbarneveldt, it made an indelible stain—though in the light of subsequent history it seems the result of panic rather than of some deep-seated murderous tendency in the Dutch people. Since 1672 the Dutch have not assassinated any of their statesmen.

CHAPTER VII

THE
PERIWIG AGE

After the flurry and exertion of most of the seventeenth century, the eighteenth century seems calm, benign, even sleepy. This age, in which the last quarter of the seventeenth century seems to fit, was one in which the Netherlands came to be visualized as the trim little land where windmills turned, tulips bloomed, the women wore strange costumes, the men drank gin, and everyone wore wooden shoes. In both the northern and southern Low Countries the eighteenth century was a stagnant period—known to the historians of the next century in the north as the *Pruikentijd*—the Periwig Age. The then fashionable powdered wigs indicated, those critics felt, a subservience to artifice at the expense of action; though of course wigs were also being worn at the time in go-ahead England and aggressive France. But certainly the energy shown by De Witt and his contemporaries had now gone, and what remained was the same rather dry, bossy manner which infused the political and artistic atmosphere of the United Provinces. The collapse of the vigorous Dutch culture of the Golden Age was quite abrupt, "an undeniable historical fact," Huizinga says. "Letter writing became bogged down in committee jargon and French phrases; schol-

Jan Wyk's portrait of William III, prince of Orange, who led the Dutch Republic against the armies of Louis XIV and later ascended the English throne

ars wrote in Latin or in Latin style, and the rest of our prose was given over to sermons." In painting, Dutch art lost much of its Netherlandish character. Such artists as Gerard de Lairesse were all for fine polish, classical ruins, and the trappings of the antique. In many ways, the Low Countries were now backwaters.

Yet there were some advantages in standing outside the turbulent mainstream. Many of the old violent passions had waned. People genuinely wanted a quiet life, as portrayed in the landscape paintings and pastoral poetry they admired. Country houses were now built along the quiet reaches of the delectable river Vecht. Merchants retired from the fray of active commerce to amuse themselves in reading and gardening and brooding about their investments. Science was considered a proper amateur occupation for men of independent means, at least in the fashionable form of acquiring specimens for a natural history collection. Other suitable gentlemanly occupations were sitting at the magistrate's bench or in a town councilor's chair. Meanwhile, money continued to roll into Dutch coffers. Sir William Temple had waxed eloquent about the Bank of Amsterdam, founded in 1609, a bank "which is the greatest treasure, either real or imaginary, that is known anywhere in the world. The place of it is a great vault under the Stadhouse, made strong with all the circumstances of doors and locks, and other appearing cautions of safety that can be." British interest in the bank remained strong, as did Dutch financial interest in Britain; in 1760 more than half the British National Debt was in Dutch hands. The English historian Charles Wilson writes: "The British Funds were quoted regularly on the Amsterdam Bourse . . . Dutch merchants, magistrates, patricians, widows, orphans and Admirals, in fact Netherlanders of every class and profession, invested in British Government securities." Business transactions between London and Russia were settled in Amsterdam, which was the clearinghouse for all Europe. Dutch financial experts worked up huge loans for governments, particularly the British, which also borrowed from the Dutch such devices as lotteries and the excise tax to pay them off again.

Although money brought the Netherlands and Britain closer and closer together—with a mail service via the Harwich-Brielle packet boat sometimes getting a Dutch letter to London in eleven hours—the other great European power was not taking a back seat. France dominated the arts and social life of the Netherlands. The Dutch theater slavishly copied French dramas. The stadholder's court at The Hague led the upper bourgeoisie in aping every whim of French fashion. James Boswell noted in 1764, while he was a student in Utrecht, "The Hague is a beautiful and elegant place. It is, however, by no means a Dutch town; the simplicity and plain honesty of the old Hollanders has given way to the show and politeness of the French." French was the language used by many men in high office, and children were taught how to correspond in French before they could write in Dutch. The leading contemporary journalist Justus van Effen, whose own early work was written in French, was impressed by the Englishmen Joseph Addison and Richard Steele, and his periodical, *Hollandsche Spectator,* attempted to lead his Dutch readers away from French affectations.

Much of this undoubtedly reflected the realities of power in the age of Louis XIV. The period 1667–1713 was one of constant pressure by the French on the southern Low Countries. Parts of Artois and many towns, including Lille, Audenarde, Courtrai, Douai, and Tournai, were taken by France. French armies occasionally penetrated the north. England and the Dutch Republic had been further brought together by the ascent of the hereditary stadholder, William III, to the British throne, following England's Glorious Revolution of 1688. England's interest was generally to prevent France from establishing herself too firmly in the Spanish Netherlands, and William led the anti-French coalition. Although Louis' generals sacked Brussels in 1695, and left the great buildings of the Grand Place in ruins (with some 3,800 houses elsewhere in the city burned as well), the Sun King's ambition to overthrow the Dutch Republic—the nation of "cheese merchants and maggots," as he referred to it—was finally thwarted. The armies of the coalition, superbly generaled by John Churchill, duke of Marlborough, and Prince Eugene of Savoy, beat the French at Blenheim, and then, in the southern Netherlands, on the fields of Ramillies, Audenarde, and Malplaquet. Peace was made by the treaties of Utrecht and Rastatt, 1713 and 1714.

Like Vienna in the nineteenth century, and Versailles and Yalta in the twentieth, Utrecht furnished one of those occasions for treaty makers to create a situation with lasting implications. While the Dutch

No. 10 't Verpakke der Haring.

No. 12 't Boete der Haring Netten.

Republic sat back exhausted from the overlarge role it had taken in the war, parts of the southern Low Countries were handed over to France forever. Louis was confirmed in his possession of Valenciennes, Cambrai, Lille, and Saint-Omer. Moreover, the greater part of the southern provinces was finally abstracted from Spain and presented once again to the Austrian Hapsburgs. The Scheldt was to remain closed, thwarting trade, and the Dutch were given the right to garrison eight towns along the French frontier at the expense of the local inhabitants—no way to popularity. Indeed, to later Belgian historians this seems the low-water mark in their national history, the moment of greatest political humiliation. It is not perhaps anachronistic to suggest that nationalist ambitions were thus inspired in the south by the presence of northern troops.

Yet for most of the century the Austrian Netherlands slumbered alongside the Dutch Republic. The Austrian government set up the Ostend Company for trading with the East Indies, but this was suppressed on account of English, French, and Dutch jealousy. Endeavor turned inward; much canal building and land reclamation went on. Flemish farming gained a progressive reputation, and English agri culturalists came to admire the rich crops of tobacco, hops, turnips, beets, potatoes, and clover. The old Flemish textile industry received a boost from the invention of the flying shuttle. Moreover, around Liège, where the prince-bishopric had remained independent of Spain and free for the most part of war devastation, industry flourished— particularly wool processing and iron production. To smelt iron, coal was now used instead of charcoal, and coal was close at hand. Coal from the deep mines of the Liège region had been regularly worked since the seventeenth century, and was exported via the Meuse through the Rijn estuary. The Meuse Valley, in fact, became the prototype of a nineteenth-century European industrial region; nails, bolts, firearms, cutlery, paper, leather, and glass were made there.

For three years during the War of the Austrian Succession (1740– 1748) the southern Low Countries had to put up with the presence of French troops, as France, with the aid of Prussia and Poland, attempted to dismember the Austrian Empire. The barrier forts (previously garrisoned by the Dutch) were dismantled. But Empress Maria Theresa's brother-in-law, Charles of Lorraine, became the ruler of the southern

Two scenes related to the Dutch herring industry are shown on these Delft plates: packing the fish, above, and repairing nets, below.

provinces when the French withdrew after the Peace of Aix-la-Chapelle (1748), and tranquillity was restored. Charles maintained a pleasure-loving court in Brussels but generally lived at the château of Tervueren. There he kept a diary full of details for stocking woods and lakes with game and fish—"I must put in my park 8 roe bucks, 150 hares, 4 woodcocks, 6 grey hens, 10 guinea fowls, 50 partridges, 100 wild ducks . . ." —and also full of the goings-on of members of his court. The duke of Arenburg was giving jewels to a dancer at the Monnaie Theater, the English minister was ruining himself over one Mademoiselle Duranay. Duke Charles drank at least a bottle of burgundy with every meal, and was a great gourmet who gave famous dinners. The Brussels churches were said to have been full of people praying for him when he was ill in 1766. Under his rule a benevolent attempt was made to educate the citizenry through the foundation of state secondary schools, not that intellectual life was particularly lively with only about 3 per cent of the population literate. Voltaire—who perhaps was not invited to court—described Brussels as "this dreary city . . . the home of ignorance, of dullness and boredom, of stupid indifference." As for the Austrian Netherlands as a whole, it was in Voltaire's eyes "an aged country of obedience, empty of wit and filled with faith." In 1760 an Austrian Netherlander named Joseph Merlin invented roller-skating.

Throughout this period foreign visitors continued to come to the northern provinces for instruction (particularly in medicine and law). The czar of Russia, Peter the Great, went through an extravagant phase of admiring the Dutch and Dutch things. He had been taught to sail in Russia by a Dutchman, and had been friendly with Dutch skippers in Archangel, imitating their dress, manners, and language. He visited Holland in 1697–98. In Zaandam, the shipbuilding port near Amsterdam, the czar tried to go native, got rid of his entourage, rented a tiny cottage, and pretended to look for a job. However, the people of Zaandam would not leave him alone. He got involved in several fist fights trying to preserve his incognito. When he went back to Russia, Peter took with him hundreds of Dutch artisans and technical experts. The Russian navy was reorganized on the Dutch model, and while he reigned Dutch was given priority in the study of foreign languages.

During the eighteenth century there were sometimes as many as four hundred foreign students in the medical school at Leiden. Many young

Scotsmen intending to be lawyers studied at Utrecht; the Dutch were then the masters of Roman law, on which Scottish law greatly depended. One who came to Utrecht, following in the steps of his grandfather and father, was James Boswell. Unlike Voltaire, Boswell thought Brussels "a gay, agreeable place," but this was perhaps in comparison with his first impression of Utrecht. He suffered a good deal from spleen, a melancholy malaise which—Sir William Temple had noted—often attacked foreigners in the Low Countries. Boswell wrote: "Holland certainly has a very harsh climate, dangerous to strangers who have been brought up in a temperate region. There are horrible fogs and excessive cold, but especially a continuous dampness,

A dazzling fireworks display held in Amsterdam on August 29, 1697, honors the official arrival of Czar Peter the Great of Russia.

except in the summer months. Thus a discontented man might describe the United Provinces, and, I confess, with considerable justice. But when one has actually made the experiment of living there, one finds that there is no great difference between Holland and other countries; that is to say, if a stranger lives well, eats well, drinks well, and dresses well—and also takes a good deal of exercise, which in Holland is absolutely necessary to give a brisk circulation to the blood and consequently an agreeable liveliness of mind. If one lives after that fashion and has a suitable occupation, one can be very well satisfied." Boswell's circulation and liveliness were improved by his acquaintance with the unconventional twenty-three-year-old daughter of a local patrician, Isabella van Tuyll, or Zélide, as she was called.

Reading Boswell, who was at this stage something of a stuffed shirt, there is little sense that within a generation Europe would be engulfed in revolution; though even Boswell was unable to avoid seeing what, in a less apathetic place, could well have been symptoms of discontent. "You meet with multitudes of poor creatures who are starving in idleness. Utrecht is remarkably ruined. There are whole lanes of wretches who have no other subsistence than potatoes, gin, and stuff which they call tea and coffee; and what is worst of all, I believe they are so habituated to this life that they would not take work if it should be offered to them." According to Boswell, if Sir William Temple had still been alive and had visited the Provinces, he would have found the alteration amazing.

Both army and navy were in a state of decay; ships in other countries were generally getting larger, but Dutch harbors silted up and became shallower. After the invasion and defeat by the French in 1747, the prestige of the United Provinces slumped severely. The oligarchy's leaders had no consistent national policy. The procrastination of delegates to the States General was a subject of sardonic humor among foreign envoys. In most towns the elders formed closed oligarchies and seldom admitted new blood. Angry riots about the practice of farming out tax collection resulted in the abolition of the practice, but did not serve to initiate any movement toward widespread reforms. In southern rural districts social conditions were distressing. The Brabant peasants, an official document of 1785 declares, "drink sour buttermilk or water, they eat potatoes and bread without butter or cheese, they are miserably

clothed, they sleep on straw. A prisoner in Holland lives better than
a peasant in Brabant."

The Dutch had no revolutionary thinkers of their own, but gradually ideas from France spread in the Low Countries as the literate inhabitants read in their Dutch- or French-language journals the writings of Montesquieu, Voltaire, and Rousseau, and also Locke and Hume. Although the Reformed churchmen followed the by now accepted pattern and added Rousseau's *Emile* and *Social Contract* to their list of forbidden books, and got the States Assembly of Holland to suppress them, as they had earlier suppressed Descartes and Spinoza, the ban no doubt attracted rather than deterred new readers.

The first indications of unrest in America went more or less unnoticed in Holland. British propaganda flooded the Low Countries after the War of Independence began, but the merchants of Amsterdam were more interested in taking commercial advantage of British problems than of backing the Americans. Bernard Vlekke says, "It was the large and enormously profitable business done at St. Eustachius [the Dutch Caribbean smuggling center] that caused the commander of the Dutch port to fire a salute to the American flag on November 16, 1776, the first foreign authority to do so." Even so, the Dutch Republic was the second country to give official recognition to the United States of America, and when the new country went looking for money, it turned naturally to Amsterdam. John Adams, arranging a loan of five million guilders, told the States General: "The originals of the two Republicks are so much alike that the history of the one seems but a transcript from that of the other, so that every Dutchman instructed in the subject must pronounce the American Revolution just and necessary, or pass censure upon the greatest actions of his immortal ancestors." And John Paul Jones, sheltered for three months in Holland in 1779 despite British protests, declared, "The Dutch people are for us and for the war."

Tempted by French bribes in the form of lower customs tariffs, the Dutch Republic stumbled into the war against Britain, on the side of America, but in complete subjection to America's ally, France. Saint Eustachius was totally ravaged by the British admiral George Rodney. The West India Company was moribund, and the East India Company fell apart, although French fleets saved the Dutch colonists in the Cape of Good Hope and Ceylon. Having lost trade, honor, and lands in India, the Dutch were glad to see the war ended at the Peace of Paris in 1784. But they did not take the opportunity for reforms of their own. Although the burghers now had a cautious interest in "democracy," and democratic clubs were founded which held congresses and parades, these middle-class Dutch were more willing to talk about the liberty of the people than to die for it. The oligarchy (the states' rights faction, led by the so-called Patriots) expended its energies in trying to out-maneuver Prince William V of Orange, who was supported by the Calvinist clergy, the peasants, the artisan class, and the magistrates, all favoring the strong central leadership of the traditional stadholder. The antistadholder coalition blamed the prince for the disastrous out-come of Dutch involvement in the American war. William retreated and the Patriots gained control of Holland. The king of Prussia thought the occasion inflammatory and sent in an army to protect his sister, the prince's wife Wilhelmina. William was restored to power but in the bloodless war the Prussian army carried away much loot and the last of Dutch prestige. Many Patriots retired to France and America. The Dutch state was evidently at its lowest ebb as the revolutionary storm broke in France in 1789.

To many Dutch historians the following thirty years are the darkest in the annals of the Netherlands. Belgian historians find the period only a little brighter. In the Austrian Netherlands reforms in the 1780s had been imposed from the top. Emperor Joseph II, whose mother and coruler Maria Theresa died in 1780, swept away many old privileges, particularly those of the Church, and modernized local government practices. He made a frontal assault on things as they were, determined (as he told the States of Brabant) that "my duty is to save you, even if it be in spite of yourselves." He had an authoritarian belief in equality; and his knowledge of what was good for his citizens, whom he intended to make equal, was based on a trip he made through the Austrian Neth-erlands in 1781, wearing plain clothes and stopping in local hostelries under the name of Count Falkenstein. Joseph II abolished all the con-templative orders. He declared marriage to be a civil contract, outside the control of the Church. Sermons were to be put under government censorship and many seminaries suppressed. He did away with the provinces and their Assemblies, and replaced them with districts, ad-

In Zaandam to study shipbuilding, Peter disguised himself as a shipwright so that he might pass freely among the common folk.

ministered by commissioners appointed by himself. (He anticipated in many ways Napoleon's system of government.) Thousands of officials, high and low, were fired. Fairs and festivals were to be "regulated" to improve the productivity of the workers. In consequence, the enlightened despot soon offended almost everybody who felt the whole established, if antiquated, order crumbling around them.

A Brussels lawyer, Henry van der Noot, led the growing protest. Local soldiery, mobilized to serve in the Austrian army, wore the revolutionary cockade formed from the colors of Hainaut, Flanders, and Brabant—the same red, yellow, and black that would become the colors of the Belgian flag. Joseph was forced to back down on his political reforms, but he stuck to his anticlerical measures. The insurrectionist movement of François Vonck, a Flemish lawyer, received great support from the clergy. Joseph decided to use force, and was met with revolution. In the following squabble between the Vonckists and Van der Noot's statists, the latter received the support of popular frenzy. The States of United Belgium proclaimed by Van der Noot and his colleagues took the form of a conservative republic—a very short-lived republic—whose constitution copied parts of the American Declaration of Independence but whose principal aim was to get rid of Joseph's reforms. In February, 1790, the Austrian army, which had retrenched in Luxembourg, regained control of the revolted provinces for their new emperor, Leopold II, though Liège promoted new disturbances. Indeed, after the fall of the Bastille, the Liegeois stormed the City Hall, threw out the prince-bishop, and urged the French to "liberate" the southern Netherlands. In 1792 the French attempted to do just this; in 1794 they succeeded. In 1795 French revolutionary armies entered Holland, accompanied by émigré members of the Dutch Patriot movement who had formed the Batavian legion. They believed the time had come to restore the old Germanic "freedoms."

Throughout the Low Countries, north and south, the nearly twenty-year period of French occupation saw growing discontent. Welcomed at first, the French were soon hated. In the southern provinces the French suppressed all the old privileges, charters, and freedoms in the name of the new liberty, equality, and fraternity. They also established an administrative and judicial system which in many respects has remained into the present day. In 1797 Austria ceded her Netherlands

provinces to France; they became departments first of the republic and
then of the Napoleonic empire. The duchy of Luxembourg, occupied
by the French 1795–1814, was named the *Département des Forets*.
Under Napoleon there was further centralization and the introduction
of the civil code, a new coinage, and a new system of weights and
measures. Taxation was heavy and military service compulsory. Church
lands were confiscated. Secondary education came under government
control. More popular were the opening of the Scheldt River and estuary to shipping for the first time since 1585, and the opening up of
France as a market for the southern provinces' nascent industry. Many
old guilds and corporations disappeared, and the restrictive practices of
others were swept away. Metal, wool, coal, and textile production was
stepped up as manufacturing advances were made. Lieven Bauwens
brought to Ghent parts of the new spinning jenny, which he had
sneaked out of England, to revolutionize cotton spinning. (The jenny
concentrated spinning in factories, taking work from the wives and
children of peasants.) William Cockerill, a British engineer from
Lancaster, built the first mechanical textile looms at Verviers and Liège.
Coke replaced charcoal in factory furnaces. So Belgium took the lead,
after England, in the Industrial Revolution.

But from 1811 resistance grew against French rule. Young men
evading conscription hid in the forests of Ardennes with the connivance
of the clergy. In the Flemish provinces where the traditional Dutch
language was forbidden in official use, hatred of the French occupation
ran high. Under the police regime imposed by Napoleon hostility was
general, and Liège the only region remaining loyal to France. During
the hundred days of Napoleon's return, Louis XVIII took refuge in
Ghent. At Waterloo soldiers of the southern provinces, after a year of
freedom from French rule, fought with the British and Prussians
against Napoleon.

Meanwhile, the former Dutch Republic experienced the dubious
delights of being France's client state, now renamed the Batavian Republic. This, from the start, involved them willy-nilly in French ambitions and French wars. The British navy blockaded the coast of Holland. In October, 1797, the Dutch fleet from Texel was sent to sea to
fight a British squadron at Camperdown. Sixteen ships fought against
sixteen, with great skill and courage on both sides. In the end the Dutch

admiral De Winter suffered a stunning defeat and surrendered, having lost half his ships. Colonies were taken from the Dutch, and at home they were forced to feed, pay, clothe, and quarter twenty-five thousand French soldiers. Under Grand Pensionary Rutger Jan Schimmelpenninck, who held office for a year, reforms in taxation and primary education were accomplished; but other frequent constitutional changes had little lasting effect. Napoleon's dynastic ambitions were soon felt. The Dutch were given the dubious choice of being annexed to France or—as happened in 1806—becoming a kingdom under Napoleon's brother Louis Bonaparte.

For three years Louis had a certain popularity in Holland. His little kingdom of Holland was not just that one province but all seven provinces of the north; moreover, the name formally recognized the preeminence of the province of Holland and gave it a further legitimacy in the eyes of foreigners who, then as now, had become used to calling the whole country of the Netherlands by the name of Holland. Louis learned Dutch, and many of the so-called Batavians entered his service. Then he fell out of favor with the emperor. Napoleon, in an attempt to undermine the British economy, had introduced his Continental system, forbidding France and its client states to do business with Great Britain. Ships—even ships of other nations—which trafficked with the enemy were refused entry into French-controlled ports. Louis Bonaparte was the first to ignore the ruling. The English had made a landing in Zeeland and the Dutch had gone on smuggling and trading with England. Napoleon thought that his brother was not strict enough with his Dutch subjects; Louis was forced to abdicate in 1810. For the next three years Holland was simply a section of the empire, administered by French officials.

In terms of efficiency and honesty, it was a period of successful government. Taxes were levied with greater fairness, justice was administered with promptness and without favoritism, the police were tough but incorrupt, and the military system worked smoothly, conscripting some fifteen thousand young Dutchmen to serve in the Grande Armée —few returned from the campaign in Russia. The Continental system was now strictly enforced. The provinces were turned into departments, and orderly methods of government introduced which long survived the occupying power that introduced them. But naturally no one en-

joyed these foreign innovations, however well they worked, and discontent was increased by severe unemployment and food shortages.

The Dutch threw off French rule in November, 1813, inspired by the news of Napoleon's defeat at Leipzig. The prince of Orange landed on the beach at Scheveningen, near The Hague. The son of William V, he assumed the title of William I, sovereign prince; but those who welcomed him seemed to think they had managed to live through the days of innovation. The prince was greeted with a proclamation: "Orange above all. . . . Everyone thanks God. The old days are returning." At the Congress of Vienna, 1814–1815, the victorious allied powers gave William a new kingdom: the provinces of the former Dutch Republic combined with the southern provinces (although for the benefit of the latter the arrangement was called a "union").

This cartoon of 1814 shows Napoleon replacing heavy casualties of his wars by recruiting mere boys—including 15,000 Dutchmen—for his ill-fated campaigns.

The kingdom of the Netherlands thus brought together the two Low Countries partners who had gone their separate ways in the late sixteenth century. It was not a unanimously popular decision. At the Congress of Vienna, Russia thought both sets of provinces should be incorporated into Prussia. The Belgians—to give them the name, harking back to the ancient Belgae, that they had now begun to favor—would rather have stayed with the Austrians or joined the French, instead of their Calvinist neighbors. (Austria, which lost the southern provinces, was compensated with lands in northern Italy, whose inhabitants were not consulted.) The great supporter of the new kingdom was Britain, which wanted a strong bulwark against France. In these circumstances, the new partners did not welcome each other with open arms. The Catholic south objected to a Protestant monarch. Although the Flemings spoke a Dutch patois, they too were mostly Catholic, and suspicious of the northern Protestants. The southerners had a million more people than the north, and thus felt they should have a majority of delegates in the States General. But the Dutch insisted that they had more experience in self-government, and fewer illiterates, which gave them the right to parity. Old wounds continued to fester. Antwerp still resented Amsterdam, which had taken away its wealth and power.

The new kingdom included the highly Francophile province of Liège but not the adjacent grand duchy of Luxembourg. To make everything even more complicated, this territory (which had lost some of its eastern districts to Prussia) was given to William I, in exchange for his hereditary rights in German Nassau. Although it was technically incorporated in the new German Confederation, the grand duchy was joined to the new kingdom of the Netherlands in a personal union under the sovereign prince. It was an artificial conjunction, for though the grand duchy had been connected to the Low Countries since the first Duke Philip of Burgundy purchased the sparsely populated mountainous land from Elizabeth, widow of John of Bavaria in 1441, it had little to do with Low Countries affairs. The duchy of Luxembourg was never included in the mysterious figurings of the Seventeen Provinces; it did not send representatives to the States General; it had no great cultural links with the Low Countries and in respect of topography it was divided from them by the Ardennes, a rugged region of forested hills. Under the 1815 treaties, Prussia had the

Hortense Bonaparte, queen of Holland from 1806 to 1810, and her children
OVERLEAF: *Wellington's troops route the French at the Battle of Waterloo.*

right to keep a garrison in the duchy. Consequently, in 1867–68, William III, king of Holland and grand duke of Luxembourg, became involved in a row between France and the North German Confederation —the Germans objected strongly to William's plan to sell his sovereignty of the supposedly now neutral and independent duchy to France.

Despite all the problems that lay between them, it looked for a while after 1815 as if the remarried couple, Holland and Belgium, might make a success of their experimental coming together again. Good father William pledged himself to bring civil and religious liberty to all the subjects of his new kingdom. New highways and canals were built; Ghent, Amsterdam, and Rotterdam gained improved connections with the sea, and Antwerp's maritime trade stirred once more. John Cockerill, of Belgium's eminent industrialist family, built blast furnaces and rolling mills with royal encouragement, and shipbuilding was revived. But the north remained apathetic despite the royal incentives. Dutch trade continued to decline and poverty was widespread— perhaps seven hundred thousand out of the total two million inhabitants in the northern provinces were dependent on charity. Colonies of distressed city folk were founded in the peat districts of Groningen and Friesland. People emigrated in larger numbers than ever before to North America.

In the south William founded in 1822 an industrial investments firm, the Société Générale, which was to become a great world-wide financial power. He invested millions of his own fortune in various projects. He set up a state education system and established new state universities at Ghent and Liège. (This gave the Catholic clergy cause for grief.) William also made a particular effort to restore the Dutch language to Flanders. In 1814, according to Pieter Geyl, the Flemish language was in a bad state. "For two centuries the Flemings had been isolated, politically and morally, from what had suddenly become the leading region in Netherlands culture, Holland. They had been all that time associated with the Walloons under the auspices of a foreign, but French-speaking court at Brussels. On top of that they had been incorporated for twenty years, from 1794 to 1814, in the French Republic and French Empire and exposed to an intensive policy of gallicization." The result was that the Dutch language in Flanders had been driven out of public life and reduced to a patois; one more reason why the proper-speaking Dutch might look down on the uncouth, papist Flemings. King William decided to change all this. He decreed that Dutch be taught and used officially in the Flemish provinces.

But to many this too seemed like another step in the Calvinist takeover. William added to the opposition by introducing measures to control the training of Catholic priests. He antagonized liberals by persecuting the editors of critical journals. Catholics and liberals together demanded limitation of the royal power, and William after some initial shilly-shallying, conceded the point by repealing many of the annoying laws. Reform, here as in France in the 1780s, was the midwife of rebellion. With the immediate example at hand of the July Revolution in Paris, in 1830, the southern provinces broke up the kingdom. The revolution began theatrically enough at the opera. On the night of August 25, 1830, the première of Auber's *La Muette de Portici* took place in Brussels. The opera was about a Neapolitan revolt against Spanish rule in 1648, and the revolutionary songs made a deep impression on the audience at the Monnaie Theater:

> *For a slave what peril counts,*
> *Better death than life in chains.*
> *Off the yoke that stifles us!*
> *Perish aliens at our hands....*
> *To my country, life I owe,*
> *And she owes me liberty!*

Suddenly they were on their feet, cheering, and within a few minutes they were re-enacting the plot of the opera in the streets of Brussels. Rioting spread from one town to another. The bourgeois revolutionaries, eager to cut loose from Holland and bathe in the progressive influence of France, were helped by unemployed workers. It was quite like the old medieval days in Flanders. The mob shouted *Viva La Belgique!* while the national guard volunteers sang *La Brabançonne,* the new anthem written by a Frenchman. William's troops, led by his son Frederick, were met by barricades. The rebels lost 1,800 dead but soon controlled the whole south save Antwerp, where William's men hung on to the fortress. A provisional government proclaimed the independence of the Belgian provinces.

CHAPTER VIII

BELGIUM AND HOLLAND: THE NINETEENTH CENTURY

Out of this revolution the southern provinces became a nation-state with a name of their own and their own king, Leopold, prince of Saxe-Coburg-Gotha. Leopold satisfied many requirements. He was a forty-year-old German nobleman who had served in the Russian army against Napoleon. In 1816 he became a British subject when he married the heiress to the British throne, Princess Charlotte—cutting out in the process King William's son, the prince of Orange, who had also been wooing Princess Charlotte. In 1830 he had already been offered and refused the throne of Greece. He was a Protestant, and sympathetic to all things English, and therefore—in the eyes of Lord Palmerston, the British foreign secretary, a good person to ensure that Belgium did not simply become a French protectorate. (Palmerston, countering the plan of the French minister Talleyrand to split up the southern provinces between France and Germany, acquired the nickname "Father of Belgium.") Moreover, in 1831 Leopold was now eligible—because his wife Charlotte had died—to marry one of Louis Philippe's daughters, and thus satisfy the French leanings of so many Belgians (though some, particularly in Antwerp—still held by the

Self-portrait of Vincent van Gogh, volatile son of a Calvinist preacher, who gave up theology for painting in 1880

Dutch—and Ghent, were for preserving the tie with Holland.) Leopold was elected king of the Belgians and was joyfully received in Brussels in July, 1831.

It was now the turn of the members of the House of Orange to have a fit of pique. King William did not like the terms of separation proposed by the great powers. His son the prince of Orange (who preferred the life of Brussels to that of The Hague) complained of Leopold, "That man has robbed me before of my wife, and now of my kingdom." He led into Belgium an army of thirty thousand men to avenge the repulse suffered the year before by Dutch troops and in a ten-day campaign completely vanquished the Belgian army. It was, one trusts, the last time the northern and southern Low Countries would go to war against each other. The great powers quickly intervened to save Leopold's new throne. A truce was arranged. But it took nearly eight years to work out a divorce settlement that suited the stubborn Dutch monarch. Boundaries were adjusted, not always with the aid of common sense. In one place a three-mile-wide strip of Dutch soil was created between Germany and Belgium. Holland kept both banks of the Scheldt estuary. Luxembourg was partitioned, half ceded to Belgium, half remaining William's personal possession. Until 1868 the province of Limburg was a member of the North German Confederation.

The long dispute over the settlement shook the affection in which King William had been held by his own subjects. The national debt of Holland had risen to the giddy height of 1,726,000 guilders, or nearly 850 guilders per inhabitant. In Belgium, on the other hand, the national debt worked out at 7.5 guilders per person. There were, then, practical reasons why the north wanted to remain linked with, and share its burdens with, the south. (The population of each country at this time was 3.5 million in Belgium, 2 million in Holland.) Moreover, resentment had built up against William's autocratic rule. He had got rid of the Council of State and had made most of his important decisions without seeking the cooperation of the States General. Much of the time his despotism had been enlightened or forceful: he prompted the foundation of the Netherlands Trading Society to revitalize the East Indies trade; he introduced a new system of economic exploitation in Java, from which great returns were anticipated; he promoted the reclamation of land, with the subsidiary intention of relieving poverty; he encouraged the introduction of steamboats on the canals and the building of the first Amsterdam-Haarlem railroad; and he foresaw a great future for Curaçao, helped by a canal that he wanted his subjects to build across Central America. However, he suffered the fate of many energetic despots, which is to be surrounded by public indifference and inchoate opposition, resented by people for the fact that he, the king, was taking so much initiative and achieving things.

Generally, despite William I, it was a low time in the history of the Dutch provinces. One Dutch historian writes of the society of the 1830s: "Its fiction was unimaginative, its poetry either pedestrian or bombastic, science straggled in the track of foreign research, art manufactured soulless academic masterpieces, drama was sentimental drivel, and music was borrowed from abroad." This stagnant age seemed to be enlivened only by the internal religious quarrels of Amsterdam scholars and rural Calvinists. In the country districts zealous Protestants made plans to secede and create a new properly orthodox Calvinist Church; attempts by the king and government to subdue the movement only caused it to flourish. A novel which conveys something of this time is Arthur van Schendel's *The Waterman* (written earlier in this century). Under the wide skies and in a watery landscape, a flat horizon broken only by the occasional steeple or barn roof, Schendel presented a religious brotherhood that has settled on the Waal River. This Brotherhood of the Prophets of a New Light was founded by a barge skipper, and many of its adherents make a living carrying goods and peat along the Netherlands waterways. The Brotherhood harks back to the earlier Low Countries sects, though the members exhibit less Messianic exaltation. They share their possessions, are opposed to violence, and try to follow in literal fashion the teachings of Christ.

A potato blight increased the general poverty. Many under the leadership of their church ministers left Holland. The towns of Holland, Michigan, and Pella, Iowa, were among the midwestern American communities founded at this time. In 1840 King William himself left Holland—he abdicated in favor of his eldest son and retired to his estates in Silesia. He died in Berlin in 1843.

In Belgium there were brighter aspects: the first achievement was a new constitution, voted by the National Congress in February, 1831. It brought Belgium with one jump into modern times insofar as the

OVERLEAF: *In "The Potato Eaters" Van Gogh depicts the hard existence of Hainaut peasants, among whom he lived and preached as a young man.*

framework of the nation was concerned, and throughout the nineteenth century was a constitutional model for many other countries. Perhaps helped by Joseph II's attempted reforms in the 1780s, the new constitution embraced such up-to-date notions as freedom of the press, freedom of association, and freedom of religious worship, while holding on to traditional liberties like freedom from arbitrary arrest and the right to own property. (In some regions the traditional liberties were of long standing. In Liège, for example, Bishop Albert de Cuyck granted a charter in 1208 which declared that the people might not be taxed without their own consent. Among other provisions, the charter freed them from the burden of lodging and feeding armed men, from being subject to trial by combat, and from being arrested for debt within eight days of Easter and Christmas.) Only those who owned a certain amount of property were granted the right to vote, so democracy was by no means total; but the elected two-chamber parliament hedged about the power of the king. Parliament had to approve his choice of ministers, and no bill could receive royal assent without parliamentary passage. His veto had to be countersigned by at least one minister. Yet within this constitution Leopold in time found plenty of elbowroom for royal maneuver. He held up bills indefinitely by not signing them, dissolved the chambers when he felt like it, and fired or appointed ministers as he saw fit. Being commander in chief of the forces enabled him to act as his own minister of war. His blood ties with many European royal families—he was called the "Uncle of Europe"—gave him great leverage in foreign affairs. So although Belgium had one of the earliest European democratic constitutions, it also had a king who maintained within it a greater authority than other European constitutional monarchs.

Belgium's industrial revolution—also earlier than that in other continental countries—continued, though with the divorce from Holland, and the loss once more of the Scheldt waterway and Dutch markets, new steps had to be taken to preserve its momentum. Steam powered the nineteenth century, nowhere more than in Belgium. John Cockerill proposed a railway system with steam engines—his firm built the first locomotives on the Continent. The first European railroad opened in May, 1835, with a run from Brussels to Malines. The railway network fostered the expansion of industry and soon served the whole country

(Belgium today has one mile of track for every 1.4 square miles of land, proportionately more than any other country in the world.) Native raw materials that were now exploited included coal, iron, zinc, sand, slate, and clay. Industrial progress was helped by the creation of large corporations, in particular commercial banks which channeled investment funds into growing industries.

This expansion, however, was not evenly distributed; the Walloon region prospered most, along the Meuse and Sambre rivers, around Mons, Charleroi, Liège, and La Louvière. In Flanders, where the cotton industry had lost its Dutch colonial market and the handicraft linen makers were suffering from English mechanical competition, the bad times were aggravated by a potato blight. Impoverished Flemings began to commute to work in Walloon industries. Indeed, the misery of Flanders was such that it became necessary to break down the tariff walls with which Belgium had protected herself; grain was now brought in free of customs duties. By 1870 Belgium was practicing a free trade policy on most items, particularly foodstuffs and raw materials. The country's own stock of raw materials clearly would not last long, but with its crossroads situation, ease of communications, and a plentiful supply of skilled workers and enterprising managers, Belgium remained a successful industrial nation. By the end of the century chemical and electrical products were being manufactured in quantity. Heavy machinery and locomotives were exported. Leopold II was a great chamber of commerce man, with worldwide financial interests of his own, and many close acquaintances among bankers and industrialists. Belgian interests had a monopoly in the public utilities and power supply in seventy-six foreign cities. Belgian capital invested in the construction of railways in Spain, Italy, China, and the Balkans. The Belgian banker and industrialist Edouard Empain built the Paris Metro, Russian railways, the Cairo tram system, and the new Egyptian city of Heliopolis. Jean Jadot financed the Compagnie du Kasai, in the Congo, and built the Peking-Hankow railroad. Other Belgian mechanics and engineers worked in South America and Russia. Following the Dutch who had drained Russian marshes and built Peter the Great's navy, the Belgians built glassworks and chemical factories; by 1900 there were 130 Belgian corporations in Russia, particularly in the Donets Basin, the "Russian Belgium."

Karl Marx spent three years in Belgium. He remarked, "It's a paradise for capitalists and hell for the working classes." A Belgian econo-
mist writes of the nineteenth century: "Partly because of the necessity
of competing on foreign markets and of keeping costs as low as possible, and partly because of the lack of unionization, the tendency of Belgian manufacturers was to keep the level of wages very low." In Britain, which had shown Belgium the way into the Industrial Revolution,
social concern was beginning by 1844 to bring about legislation con-
cerning the running of factories; but in Belgium an inquiry in 1846
into the state of the poor revealed great poverty and had little practical
effect. Children worked long, hard hours. The poor ate mostly potatoes.
Unions were slow to get started and socialist groups in such industrial
centers as Ghent and Verviers were constrained from joint action by
the language barrier—as always a constant irritant and impediment between the Flemings and Walloons. A long depression occurred in the
1870s and 1880s, with consequently severe unemployment. In 1867
the collieries of Charleroi and the Borinage (where Vincent van Gogh
lived for several years as a lay preacher, and painted the people) went
on strike; eighteen workers were shot. Mass rallies led to the recognition of embryonic unions; in the beginning they took the form of mutual benefit societies, which ran shops, restaurants, hospitals and—important in beer-drinking Belgium—breweries. Out of this movement
emerged the Belgian Labor Party in 1885. It advocated public ownership of the means of production but confirmed the rights of individuals to own private property. What the party wanted for the people
seems ordinary enough now: free education for all, the legalization of
trade unions, shorter working hours, employer's liability for accidents,
and an income tax as a fairer method of levying revenue for the state.

In the same year the Charleroi miners struck for a ten-hour day;
glassworkers in the vicinity of Seraing hoisted the red flag and destroyed machinery. Troops moved into the provinces of Hainaut and
Liège. Thousands of workers marched in protest in Brussels. In 1893
a general strike was called to demand universal suffrage, for at this
time only 137,000 could vote out of a six-million population. Twenty
workers died in the rioting, and results were not long in coming. Various Catholic-dominated ministries brought about a series of reforms
over the next few decades—pensions, accident insurance, minimum

*Flower vendors hawk their wares in front of a distillery in late-nineteenth-
century Brussels.*

wages, and low-cost housing for workers, among other things. At last Sunday became a compulsory holiday for all. Nightwork for women and children was banned. All men over the age of twenty-five were given the vote after the 1893 general strike—only some, with better educational qualifications than others, had more than one vote. Unions gained further recognition, although it was 1921 before they achieved the substance and legality they sought.

A similar progress toward social democracy went on in the Netherlands, with some aspects gained earlier, some later than in Belgium. It took time for the country to recover from the profound depression in agriculture in the 1840s. Other millstones hanging around Holland's neck were land scarcity, an obsolete fleet of merchant ships, and fishing encumbered by medieval regulations. But between 1840 and 1860 import duties on raw materials were gradually abolished, and after 1860 Dutch industry picked up, particularly as a result of the growth of Ruhr Valley industries. This brought about a big increase in barge trade on the Rijn. In eastern Overijssel cotton manufacture boomed as cotton goods found an excellent market in the Indies. Tilburg, the Brabant town which had inherited Leiden's wool industry, and Maastricht, with its ceramic works, were among the towns that now began to prosper, as the industrial revolution arrived later than elsewhere. By the end of the century the electrical firm of Philips was established at Eindhoven. Capital was available once more for investment—in Russia, central Europe, and in the United States. Amsterdam banks lent funds to Southern states for reconstruction after the Civil War.

On succeeding his father in 1840, William II set up a committee to work on the reform of the constitution. The Netherlands became a parliamentary monarchy, in which the king had less and less say and liberal measures began a gradual undermining of conservative stolidity. The mid-century generation of artists and men of letters still looked backward. Perhaps one of its liveliest products—because it has some wit—is a poem by Petrus de Genestet, hailing his homeland:

> O, land of mud and mist, where man is wet and shivers,
> Soaked with humidity, with damp and chilly dew,
> O, land of unplumbed bogs, of roads resembling rivers,
> Land of umbrellas, gout, cold, agues, toothache, flu,

O, spongy porridge-swamp, O, homeland of galoshes,
Of cobblers, toads and frogs, peat diggers, mildew, mould,
Of ducks and every bird that slobbers, splutters, splashes,
Hear the autumnal plaint of a poet with a cold. . . .

It was a dull, narrow-minded time, when many historic monuments and city walls were razed, and nothing very enterprising replaced them.

Among the mass of people wages of one guilder a day were common. Indirect taxes placed an unfair burden on the working classes. The first social legislation—a bill restricting child labor, came in 1874, and the franchise was gradually extended. Because tax qualifications allowed only certain males over age twenty-five to vote, the electorate in 1870 consisted of a hundred thousand men in a population of three and a half million. In 1887 men with a better education were given the benefit of lower tax qualifications. As time went on, prosperity and wider education increased the proportion of voters but also increased the de-

The Belgian James Ensor presents a macabre scene in "Skeletons Disputing"
recalling the nightmarish vision of such early Flemish masters as Bosch.

mand for votes for all men and women without hindrance; all Dutch men got the vote in 1914, the women in 1922.

Both northern and southern Low Countries were much affected by their colonies. In mid-century the Dutch at home were kept going by income from Java plantations—in 1849, the Indies provided 20 million guilders of the 70 million guilders budget; they were, as one commentator of the time said, "the cork that kept the Netherlands afloat." Holland got back its island territories from the British in 1816, and in the course of the nineteenth century Dutch power was extended through Java, the Moluccas, Sumatra, the Celebes, and almost the entire Indonesian archipelago. For five years the Javanese fought a guerrilla war against the Dutch. The Russian ambassador in Brussels wrote to his government: "They avoid battles with the troops and have adopted a plan of undermining the strength of the Europeans with the help of the unhealthy climate and fatigue." In the end the Dutch captured the guerrilla leader. It is reckoned that in the Java war 200,000 Javanese were killed plus 8,000 Dutch and 7,000 Indonesian mercenaries. Until 1877 Javanese farmers were forced to hand over to the government part of their lands and one fifth of their work time. The government could also tell them what crops it wanted grown. Under this system profits were large and the native agricultural workers hard pressed.

The system was also responsible for the first vigorous Dutch novel of the century: *Max Havelaar,* written under a pseudonym by a former East Indian government official, Eduard Douwes Dekker. *Max Havelaar* (1860) was a fierce attack on the exploitation of the Indies, and it prepared the ground for those who wanted to reform the system of forced-labor farming. Public opinion changed: the Indies ceased to be thought of simply in terms of profit and humor. Reforms took place. Compulsory production was abolished, and to protect the poor peasantry ownership of the soil was to be determined by native customary law. After 1877 East Indian budget surpluses were no longer remitted to the Netherlands but were reinvested in island administration, roads, schools, public health, and irrigation. Much of this colonial empire was ruled (under the mostly benevolent overall sovereignty of the Dutch) by native princes. One prince who resented the Dutch overlordship was the sultan of Atjeh, in northern Sumatra. For almost forty years a state of war existed between Batavia and Atjeh.

The Dutch were not just absentee landlords; they settled in Indonesia and governed their huge island empire with the help of sea power. Many Dutch who made Indonesia their home, and who often took Indonesian wives, had an unself-critical sense of being natural masters of the islands. They were certainly unsympathetic toward the inevitable rise of nationalist movements, although their administration remained mostly indirect, delegated to the traditional village governments, and interfered little with Indonesian religion and culture. For unlike the Catholic Portuguese, the Dutch had no ambition to save the souls of the Indonesians; they were interested primarily in profit. Even without the return of direct revenues, the Indies brought to Holland the benefits of trade, making the Dutch the third or fourth largest colonial power. The Indies were not just the Spice Islands now, but supplied tin, rubber, kapok, oil, and cigar wrappers, and were of course a market for Dutch goods. The islands also gave the Dutch the smug satisfaction of empire-owning. In The Hague colonial merchants and former colonial officials built their prosperous houses and lived close, materially comfortable lives—although, as is demonstrated brilliantly in Louis Couperus' novel *Old People and the Things That Pass* (1906), the experience of the Indies had added an element that would always unsettle them. Certainly the Indies warmed these cold people of the north, and enlivened them with their spices.

Belgium owed its colonial empire to its kings. Leopold I wanted an empire to match those acquired by countries ruled by his relatives, and during his reign he attempted to start trading posts in Guatemala, Abyssinia, and Guinea. At his death he passed on this imperial ambition to his son. Leopold II, disappointed by an initial search after he came to the throne in 1865, began to look in Africa. Under his sponsorship Sir Henry Morton Stanley led an expedition into the Congo, using Leopold's yacht, the *Royal,* and not hesitating to apply tough methods against the natives to get through the bush. At first Leopold worked behind the Association Internationale du Congo, whose blue flag Stanley planted over a great region of subequatorial Africa; but even when the great powers of Germany, France, and Britain (who were carving up Africa) realized who was the real backer of this venture, it suited them to forego their own ambitions in the Congo and allow an outside party to possess it. Leopold was recognized as head of the Congo Free

State, which would be connected with Belgium only through its ruler.

The Congo was eighty times bigger than Belgium. To open it up Leopold put at risk his private fortune and in the first years went deeply in debt. This perhaps was one factor that led him to allow the development of a punitive system; a tax in the form of labor was imposed on the natives. The agents of Leopold's state were empowered to buy ivory and rubber from the Congolese at state-fixed prices. The agents also got a commission on all ivory and rubber so acquired.

The system clearly led to abuses. Although Leopold promoted research in tropical medicine, forbade the sale of alcohol to the natives (for whom, however, a good drunk might have alleviated some of their troubles), and put down the slave trade, he was concerned to make his empire pay and to keep out all competitors. And though King Leopold knew what was happening, and was undoubtedly responsible for the savage cruelty imposed in his personal domain, the Belgians themselves could not be altogether exonerated. E. D. Morel, leader of the Congo Reform Society in Britain, wrote in 1909, "Sections of the (Belgian) upper and middle class secured handsome returns; contractors did a flourishing business for a time; much wealth accrued to Antwerp in particular. Never was wealth so demonstrably the produce of systematized evil-doing. There were none of the intermediate stages which confuse issues and defy detection by the difficulty of tracing cause and effect. In this case cause and effect were separated only by the extortion of the raw material from the natives, accompanied by wholesale massacre and by every species of brutal outrage which diseased minds could invent, the unloading of that raw material upon the Antwerp quays, and the disposal of it on the market." The profits of the Congo identified the Belgians in fact, if not in law, with a criminal form of colonial exploitation; and those profits were eventually paid for. "Leopold had replaced the natives' fear of the slaver with fear of the white man," writes Colin Legum, an expert on contemporary Africa. "It is one of the embedded roots in the Congo's disaster."

By 1895 Leopold's Congo property was returning a profit (three million pounds during the period 1896–1906). But also in 1895 an American named J. B. Murphy told the press that Africans in the equatorial area were often shot if they did not produce enough rubber. Protestant ministers reported atrocities: murder, mutilation, and extortion. The

Leopold II, king of Belgium from 1865 to 1909, who reaped a huge personal fortune through exploitation of the Congo Free State

British consul at Boma and the Italian consul at Matadi backed up the reports (as, for modern readers, Conrad's *Heart of Darkness* still does). In Europe and the United States there were demands for the Congo to be taken out of Leopold's hands. The king's own commission of inquiry supported the missionaries' charges. In Belgium there had been a feeling among many that they did not want to tangle with the Congo problem—socialists did not approve of colonialism, and monarchists wanted to abide with the king's desire to have the state inherit the Congo after his death and remained passive. But slowly Belgians got over these inhibitions. In 1908 the Belgian government voted to annex the Congo Free State, which thus became the Belgian Congo.

Leopold II died a year later, unloved despite the widespread improvements—boulevards, museums, public gardens—he lavished on Brussels and other Belgian communities in his years of wealth. In the Congo the tax in the form of labor was abolished, the state monopoly set aside, and competitive trade encouraged. The administration remained paternal, by royal decree with the advice of an expert council and the approval of parliament. But colonial-studies courses were established in Brussels and Louvain. The Catholic Church was given the responsibility of educating the Congolese. The bargain struck between Leopold II and the Vatican in 1906 called for perpetual grants of land and subsidies to the Catholic missions in return for their provision of schools. The curriculum, however, had to be approved by the government. Judged by the light of other African colonies, the Congo within a few decades had a high literacy rate.

At home in Belgium religion and education formed a divisive issue through much of the century. Both Catholics and liberals wanted the education system to put forward their own views. Louvain was reestablished as a Catholic university in 1834, and the Freemasons set up the University of Brussels to compete with it. The Church kept a strong grip on rural schools despite successive attempts by liberal governments to shake it loose. The Catholic bishops prohibited their flocks from attending the new state secondary schools. There were anticlerical riots. The writings of Auguste Comte and Charles Darwin encouraged young liberals to dismiss religion as so much hocus-pocus, while many Catholics took refuge from "progress" in mystical cults, such as the Sacred Heart. Most towns and villages had separate tradesmen catering to each

Belgium's record of colonial rule in the Congo was marred by instances of inhumanity, as shown in this photograph of a captive Congolese.

group. Parades clashed. Liberals wore cornflowers and Catholics wore poppies, for no one wanted to be taken for a member of the rival party. In the late 1870s a new law required the communes to provide secular schools with optional religious instruction in out-of-school hours, and this provoked a fierce Catholic backlash. For twenty years after 1884, Catholic ministries ruled the country, and the communes were allowed to choose between lay or Catholic schools, both state subsidized.

In Holland Catholics had the assistance of the Calvinists in their struggle against secular education. Despite the traditional association of Calvinism with the Dutch state, the Catholics at this time formed roughly 35 per cent of the population of the Netherlands. The Calvinists continued to distrust popery, but they welcomed the papists in the fights against liberal godlessness and for Christian schools and a Christian foundation of the state. Not that they thought joint action should be carried too far. Mixed marriages were generally abhorred by Calvinists and Catholics alike, and a law of 1853 stipulated that churches should not be built closer than 420 feet from each other—in order to keep the congregations at a safe distance and preserve the peace.

One boundary which the international conferences had not adjusted was the language frontier. It still ran through the Low Countries on roughly the same path it had followed since A.D. 600, after the Frankish settlement. It left the coast near Adinkerke and ran south to Armentières, along the border between France and West Flanders; then eastward via Brussels to the Dutch border near Maastricht. All above the frontier—West Flanders, East Flanders, Antwerp, Limburg, and North Brabant—is Dutch- (i.e., Flemish-) speaking. All below it—Hainaut, South Brabant, Namur, Liège, and the province of Luxembourg—is Walloon, or French-speaking. On the eastern edge of the province of Liège a majority speak German.

So the linguistically anomalous situation persists where (as Pieter Geyl has pointed out in *Debates with Historians*) the "Dutch State comprises not quite two thirds of the Dutch-speaking people in the Low Countries." The others are in the Flemish half of Belgium. Geyl writes that the nineteenth century was "a period of profound humiliation for Flanders." William I had attempted—following the French occupation—to restore something of Flemish cultural life, but the post-1830 era saw French again supreme. Flemish was not to be used in the

Belgians from Courtrai employ the time-honored method of soaking their flax in the river Lys to prepare it for spinning.

administration, law, armed services, universities, or secondary schools. Even so, many Flemings had felt antagonistic toward William when he was trying through educational reforms to rescue the Flemish language from the confusion of rural dialects into which it had fallen. They distrusted him because he was a Protestant and because his officials tended to be Dutchmen rather than Flemings. The complexities of the language problem were not lessened by the fact that most educated Flemings—seeking advancement in the government or their professions—chose to speak French and have their children taught French. At the end of the nineteenth century the leading French-speaking writers in Belgium—men such as Charles de Coster, Camille Lemonnier, and Emile Verhaeren—were all Flemings. An elite was created, divided from the Flemish majority which spoke no French at all.

Meanwhile, a Flemish movement was underway. A revival took place of Flemish literature, history, and folklore, and concurrent demands arose for full equality for the Flemish language. However, the liberals, who were mostly from the Walloon French-speaking provinces, were opposed to anything that would make the Flemings less susceptible to the up-to-date message of the French Revolution and nineteenth-century progress; from the Walloon point of view, the Flemings were too pokey and provincial as it was. But slowly the Flemish claims were acknowledged. During the 1870s Flemish became compulsory in Belgian administrative and court proceedings north of the language boundary. In 1883 it was made a compulsory subject in Flemish secondary schools. And in 1898 it became an official language of the Belgian kingdom: coins, public inscriptions, and the king's oath had now to be in both French and Flemish. The country's motto was in duplicate (and somewhat double-edged): *L'Union fait la force—Eendracht maakt macht* (Union makes strength). Perhaps in Flanders the Flemings now played down their own traditional disunity—for instance, the constant competition between the medieval towns, as when Ghent helped English troops storm Ypres, or when the guildsmen of Bruges aided Count Louis de Maele against the men of Ghent.

The last decades of the nineteenth century were a bright time for the arts of both Holland and Belgium. At The Hague during the 1880s there developed a school of excellent naturalistic painters—the three Maris brothers, Johannes Bosboom, Hendrik Willem and Sientje Mes-

A European outpost at the mouth of the Congo, as seen by a nineteenth-century Italian traveler

dag, and Jozef Israels, among others. Johan Jongkind, adopted by the French, brought to impressionism the breezy, showery Low Countries light. Moreover, between 1880 and 1885 Vincent van Gogh, having decided to devote his life to painting, turned out several hundred works influenced by the huge skies and heavy earth of Nuenen, North Brabant, where his father was pastor. Van Gogh had no school around him, and neither colleagues nor customers for his paintings; but his works have the radiance of a powerful obsession. Hendrik Berlage's authoritative brick architecture began to impress his countrymen. Eighteen-eighty is also the year in which—leaving aside *Max Havelaar*—Dutch literature woke up for the first time since the seventeenth century. Poets and little magazines took seriously first Art for Art's Sake, and then socialism. Louis Couperus delineated the tight social world of The Hague in novels which—unlike much of the poetry of the time—can still be appreciated by the foreign reader.

In Belgium, Guido Gezelle purveyed a Gothic lyricism in Flemish while the vehicle of Maurice Maeterlinck's somewhat misty mysticism was French. Unbound by language, in architecture and design, Victor Horta and Henry van de Velde formed the vanguard of *art nouveau,* and such painters as James Ensor, Rik Wouters, Henri Evenepoel, and Constant Permeke proved with original, forceful art that the country of Van Eyck, Memling, and Rubens was by no means dead.

There were as the nineteenth century drew to a close frequent reminders that the Low Countries still formed a margin of Europe, an always accessible plot of ground, where greater powers could interfere if they felt like it. Germany, after centuries as a collection of states and principalities, was now becoming a purposeful and aggressive power. In the 1870s, on the eve of the Franco-Prussian war, Otto von Bismarck revealed a secret document in which—like Talleyrand earlier—Napoleon III proposed that France should annex Belgium and Germany annex Holland. Prime Minister Gladstone of England was furious at this and made both Germany and France renew their guarantees of Belgium's neutrality. At the same time William III and Napoleon III had been dickering over the grand duchy of Luxembourg, which William owned personally, and thus could sell to Napoleon, or so he thought. But Prussia still kept a garrison in Luxembourg under the treaties of 1815, and as soon as it was clear there might be war over the proposed sale, William backed out of the arrangements. For the most part the Dutch practiced a foreign policy of constant conciliation and arbitration, which they thought befitted their position as a small power. Passive neutrality or Dutch diffidence was only threatened once, when blood ties with the South African farmers of Dutch extraction were called on during the Boer War of 1899–1902. But the liberal government of the time let economic considerations outweigh sentiment. It felt there was no point in upsetting the Boers' enemy, the British, when British naval power had such influence on Dutch interests in Asia.

The Great Powers did not see the Low Countries as a unit. In Germany there were indications that some thought the Netherlands was merely a sundered section of the North German Confederation, which ought to be given every opportunity to reconnect itself to the fatherland. Kaiser Wilhelm II imagined the German and Dutch fleets sailing together, "the flags of the House of Orange and the House of Brandenburg flying side by side on the oceans as in the days of old!" The Dutch knew such days had never been, and they had little desire to have them crop up in the future. While German generals discussed the advisability of occupying the Dutch coast and British diplomats speculated as to whether the Dutch would allow the passage of German troops into Belgium and France, the Dutch themselves set up a system of defense, based on a line of purposefully flooded countryside in the province of Utrecht. This, it was hoped, would forestall an overland invasion. The army was reorganized and neutrality emphasized.

Meanwhile, as the arms race among the Great Powers proceeded, the Belgians fortified the Meuse Valley between Liège and Namur, which had seen centuries of war, and trusted in the international guarantees of their neutrality. While on a trip to Germany in January, 1904, King Leopold II received a secret offer from the Kaiser. Wilhelm now had the romantic vision of recreating the medieval duchy of Burgundy, including the French Artois and Ardennes. This he proposed to give to Belgium in return for Belgian help in a German war against France. But there were no such fancy promises ten years later. Then the reality was a German ultimatum on August 2, 1914, demanding the right for her armies to cross Belgium into France. The demand was refused. France and Britain stood by their guarantees to protect Belgium, and the Great War began.

CHAPTER IX

WORLD WARS
AND BETWEENTIMES

T wenty-eight years may not grant much in the way of historical perspective, but from the vantage of the present day the period from 1914 to 1944 appears to have a unity. World wars frame the interim years of the roaring twenties and the depressed thirties in which none of the great problems of Europe came any closer to solution. The Second World War now seems like an echo of the First. There were differences, of course, and among them the fact that in the Second World War all three of the Low Countries were invaded, in the First, Holland managed to remain neutral. The German armies in 1914 moved round the southern tip of Limburg, perhaps because the German general staff believed there was an advantage in keeping the Netherlands out of the war. But the Belgians refused to grant passage to the Germans, thus preventing them from making a quick swoop into France. After a few months the Belgian forces under King Albert had been pushed back into West Flanders, where the Yser River runs near the French border. They stuck to this thin stretch of land through the next four years, giving Belgium a place in the bloodiest, muddiest campaign ever fought.

Those four harrowing years of battle left Western man suffering

H. de Groux's painting "Gas Warfare" depicts masked soldiers of the sort that fought on Belgian battlefields during World War I.

from collective shell shock. The war was like a medieval dance of death, large-scale. The ground of Flanders was soon full of holes and could have been compared to a giant sieve if the water had drained away—only with rain falling on the average every other day on the impervious clay soil the water stayed; the ground was always saturated. Soon too there was stalemate between the opposing armies; great masses of troops faced each other in the dubious shelter of trenches and dugouts. Artillery pounded the already pulverized ground day and night. Gas, mines, tanks, and the newfangled airplane did not bring a speedy end to the slaughter. Barbed wire and machine guns halted the Somme offensive of 1916 in France, when both sides lost some 1,250,000 men. The front stretched 350 miles from Switzerland to Ostend on the coast; in Flanders, there was grim news once more from places fought over in the fourteenth century: Ypres, the 350-foot-high Mont Kemmel, and Zillebeke. The Low Countries were never favorite fighting ground for soldiers. Alba had said, "Holland is as near to hell as possible," and Marlborough in the early 1700s commented, "Our armies swore terribly in Flanders." Now the punishment was general, affecting men and matter. The medieval Cloth Hall of Ypres, one of the glories of Flemish architecture, was blasted away. During the 1917 campaign in Flanders, which lasted roughly fourteen weeks and gained for the Allies a few miles of the Passchendaele ridge which breaks the monotonous, flat Flemish plain, some 150,000 British soldiers and perhaps twice as many German defenders were lost in rain, mud, and gunfire. The German general Erich Ludendorff wrote: "It was no longer life at all. It was mere unspeakable suffering." If generals wrote that, what did the privates say?

In occupied Belgium the Germans deported many industrial workers and their machinery. Railroads were destroyed, half the country's cattle killed, and much of its farmland laid waste. Some food came in from abroad—the British eased their blockade and neutral relief supplies got through, mitigating what otherwise might have been a famine situation. Against the Germans there were strikes and underground action. In order to divide and rule, the Germans encouraged the Flemish-Walloon quarrel, but though a few Flemings made common cause with the Germans, most—despite their impatience with the prewar Belgian state and Walloon hegemony within it—were loyal to their government and held back their dissatisfaction until the war ended.

In Holland neutrality worked, but only just. Four years of army mobilization placed a heavy financial burden on the country, and in the first part of 1918, when it was still winter, acute hunger among the city poor caused outbreaks of violence. Revolutions had recently erupted in Russia and Germany. In the streets of Amsterdam crowds rioted, and Queen Wilhelmina (who had come to the throne in 1898) personally appeared in an attempt to calm them. A socialist *Putsch* failed, and some rioters were shot by soldiers.

After the armistice, Holland had to endure a period of unpopularity. Kaiser Wilhelm had taken refuge there, and the Dutch government refused to extradite him. There were Belgians who demanded Great Power support for the annexation of Limburg, the Dutch Zeeland region of Flanders, and the half of Luxembourg they had parted with in 1839. This aggrandizement was not allowed. A plebiscite in Luxembourg in 1919 rejected the idea of total annexation by Belgium. However, since 1921 Luxembourg and Belgium have maintained an economic union. The Belgian franc is the official currency in the grand duchy, and the two countries are one as far as customs duties are concerned. The only territory Belgium gained after the First World War was a sliver of Germany near Liège.

Before the end of the First War the Netherlands had set in motion another, more peaceful, scheme for territorial growth—a costly twentieth-century campaign against the invading sea. The general in charge was Dr. Cornelius Lely, and the object was not only to repel the sea but to gain living room and farming land. Lely proposed to join North Holland and Friesland with a dike across the wide mouth of the Zuider Zee; then, in the enclosed lake so formed, to drain one by one the nine hundred square miles of polders that would be created within the lake. Ships no longer bustled about the Zuider Zee as they had done in the past. The once-flourishing ports of Enkhuizen and Hoorn had become sleepy little towns with small fishing fleets. The eel trade between Workum and London had expired, and Staveren no longer sent its ships to the Baltic. Clearly the fishermen's sons would have to become farmers.

The nineteen-mile-long Afsluitdijk, or enclosing dam, was completed on May 28, 1932; in the years following, the lake has been divided into large parcels, each parcel surrounded by a dike, and then the water drained away. The land, visible for the first time in centuries, was then planted with a series of temporary crops which improve the soil for arable cultivation—though the need for farm land is now coming second to the need to accommodate in new towns the tightly packed people of Holland. (The farmers' sons have a choice of becoming engineers, artists, or appliance mechanics.) So far Wieringen polder and the northeastern and the eastern Flevoland polders have been completed; southern Flevoland has recently emerged from the shallow waters of IJsselmeer, as the Zuider Zee is now called; and the Markerwaard, fifth and last of the great polders, is outlined on the charts for future completion. Subsidiary benefits lie in new transportation routes across the polders and in the road (joining Friesland and North Holland) across the enclosing dam; a statue of Lely marks the mid-point of the dam roadway. The reclamation has also involved shortening the coastline, and many areas are safe from the old terror of flood.

The time between the wars falls, broadly, into the booming twenties and the tense thirties. During the first period prosperity in Holland was helped by the continued growth of Rotterdam as a transit port for Dutch, German, and central European goods, and by increased profits from East Indian enterprises. In 1926 agriculture in the Indonesian archipelago paid dividends of 187,000,000 guilders, mostly to Dutch owners and managers. Nearly a hundred million guilders was paid by the East Indian government in pensions and leave allowances, and most of this money came back to the Netherlands. The Dutch made greater investments in the islands—investments which paid huge profits while the boom lasted. Such big Dutch firms as Philips, Shell, and Rotterdam shipbuilding yards continued to expand. In Belgium, following a severe bout of inflation, and devaluation in the early 1920s, a boom began, and new industries were established on the basis of products from the Congo: among others, coffee, palm oil, and copper.

Relations between Belgium and Holland were not good-neighborly in this period. Liège and Antwerp were linked by a new canal which avoided Dutch territory. The Dutch were scared that the Belgians intended to ruin Rotterdam. Bad feelings persisted even when definite steps were taken to make things right. In 1932, by the Treaty of Ouchy-Lausanne, the two countries took note of their common interest and

An austere armchair, designed in 1917 by architect Gerrit Rietveld, a leading figure of the De Stijl movement

proximity by beginning to reduce duties. However, Belgium's 1920 military alliance with France was considered by the Dutch to make the southern Low Country little more than a French pawn in European power politics. This feeling persisted even though the Belgians renounced the French alliance in the mid-thirties, because of strong Flemish antagonism to it; for that matter, even the Walloon Belgians were aware that the French tended to look down on them as uncouth country cousins. In the thirties, when Hitler was re-arming Germany and making little secret of the great ambitions of the Third Reich, little cooperation or coordination of defense efforts took place between Holland and Belgium. As late as 1940 the Dutch and Belgian military staffs viewed each other with such suspicion that they exchanged no information until after the Germans attacked. Subsequently there was no concerted action between the Dutch and Belgian armies.

Within Belgium, the pro-French policy had—as in the days when the counts of Flanders gave fealty to the French king—caused dissension. Many Flemings thought it signaled the coming destruction of their language and separate Flemish culture. A new Flemish movement called the Front Party was set up to oppose the prevailing Francophilia and repulse those considered to be the oppressors of their "race." The Flemish clergy backed this movement, which had the motto *Alles voor Vlaanderen, Vlaanderen voor Christus* (All for Flanders, Flanders for Christ). France was the land of atheism. The Flemings sang their own *Lion of Flanders* anthem instead of the Belgian *Brabançonne*. Yet the thirties brought some advantages for the Flemings. The country's language frontier was given official status and in both regions the official rights of each language were safeguarded. For education, the law, the armed services, and government, Flemish was to be used north of the frontier and French in the Walloon area to the south of it. In Brussels both languages had equal status. In each region, schools were to give instruction in the language of the other region—and this language was to have priority over any foreign language. Ghent University became a solely Flemish language institution. In fact, although the Flemings were not completely satisfied, they felt they had achieved the chance of equal education for their children, who could now study in their own tongue through the university level, and get into professions and jobs that had been closed to them hitherto.

Along the Flemish coast, the seaside towns and villages now began to sprawl—ugly concrete and discordant brick; and even on the empty land between those places, the ground seemed to have been turned into sites and lots, useful for nothing but more of the same shabby development. The bumpy brick and cobbled roads, fringed with sand, seem intended to mortify bicycle racers. The Belgian painters of this time—Paul Delvaux, René Magritte—are able to bear reality only by seeing in it the weird and fantastic; brilliant art, but entirely without joy. The paintings of Leon Spillaert are perhaps less dated, lacking the harsh and sometimes self-indulgent juxtapositions of surrealism; but Spillaert too has a sense of all-pervading loneliness and melancholy; we are all solitary figures on beaches.

These are aspects of life that George Simenon, born in Liège, catches so well, in economical evocation, in many of his brilliant books. This great Low Countries writer has lived in Paris, Arizona, Connecticut, and Switzerland, but perhaps it is particularly in his nondetective novels that life seems so morbid and burdensome, so "Belgian"; while in his Inspector Maigret books, where the darker, criminal facts are necessarily hidden or camouflaged from the reader, and Paris has its own enchantments, life is allowed to be pleasurable and wonderful. (Perhaps it is no accident that Jacques Brel, the popular post-World War II Belgian singer and composer, is alive and well and living in Paris.)

The Depression came, hitting hard. The Belgian government was at first as lethargic as others in the face of the sudden crash and international retreat into protectionism. Workers' wages had for some years been pegged to the cost of living, but now wages were cut drastically. Strikes were of little effect in a time of such widespread unemployment. In Holland, the collapse of the economies of other countries had an eventual effect, though the slump came a little later than elsewhere. As the East Indies lost many of the customers for their goods, so revenues to the mother country fell—in 1933 they were down drastically to 10 per cent of the predepression level. Since the collapse of the German economy was perhaps the most important factor, Holland tried to limit its exports to Germany after 1934, to lessen its dependence—and also to ensure that the Germans did not run up huge debts they might not honor if war began. There was no famine in the Netherlands, but half a million were out of work and there was enough dis-

OVERLEAF: *Paul Delvaux's excursions into surrealism produced such paintings as "Penelope" of 1946, whose image evokes modern man's isolation.*

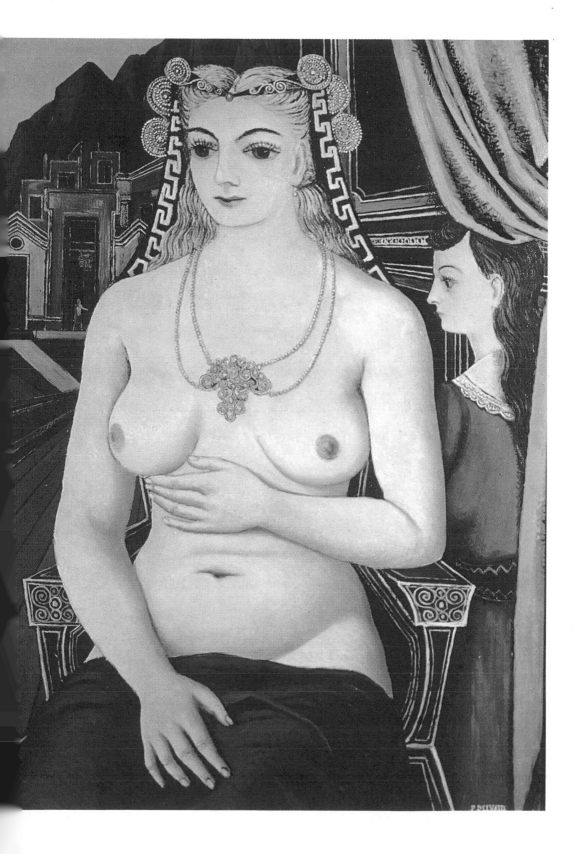

tress to cause the government to take relief measures. The government managed to put off devaluation longer than most other European countries—Holland was the last nation to abandon the gold standard—but this made prewar Holland an expensive place for tourists, and kept many away.

Despite all this, Holland at the end of the thirties had reasons for satisfaction. Prosperity was not rampant, but it was more generally enjoyed than at any earlier time in history. Adriaan Barnouw writes: "There were no glaring contrasts between excessive wealth and abject poverty. The land was dotted with prosperous villages and towns whose inhabitants, made mobile by bicycles and automobiles, built their homes ever farther away from the centers, until the countryside, especially in the densely populated western part, began to assume the aspect of a huge garden city. Co-operatives flourished in the agricultural districts and made it possible for the individual farmer . . . to dispose of his dairy and agricultural products at prices that gave him an ample compensation for his labors." The out-of-doors now provided beaches, camping sites, and parks for holidays. People's health was better than ever before. Extensive social security arrangements, such as health insurance, came during the Second World War.

In Belgium social legislation in the twenties had brought about the eight-hour working day, plans for low-cost housing, compulsory old-age insurance, and an equitable income tax. In the late thirties measures were passed for the forty-hour work week and compulsory health and unemployment insurance. In both countries politics were confusingly fragmented; leaders shifted fast. In Holland there were many small parties, long ministerial crises, and a moot question as to whether government was passive or paralyzed. In this situation, Holland and Belgium were both fortunate in their monarchies, and the people of Luxembourg seemed happy with their Grand Duchess Charlotte. The Dutch had a queen, Wilhelmina, who reflected their own preoccupation with home and was similarly devoted to domestic duties. If she was a bit rigid and matriarchal, so were many of her countrywomen. In 1938 Holland celebrated the fortieth anniversary of Wilhelmina's coming to the throne. The Belgians had a royal family that was suited to their somewhat more volatile temperament. Their King Albert was respected by socialists, monarchists, and ardent Flemings alike, but he

An up-to-date Low Countries map, indicating provinces and national boundaries

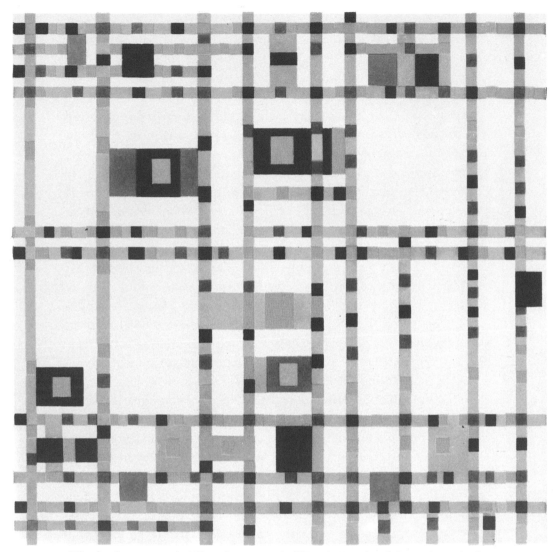

The lively, geometric "Broadway Boogie-Woogie," painted in 1942-1943 by the Dutch artist Piet Mondrian during his wartime residence in New York

died in a mountain-climbing accident in 1934, and his son Leopold III became king of the Belgians. Leopold's Swedish wife, Astrid, died in a car crash not long after her husband came to the throne; she had been greatly loved by the Belgians and some to this day still hang her photo in their living rooms. Although the Belgian Crown had a little more power than most European constitutional monarchies, it gained strength from the affection in which it was held and the need for it as a symbol of unity among a querulous and often divided people.

Whatever radicalism there was in prewar Holland seemed to express itself in painting and design. A new movement—which took the name De Stijl—demonstrated a frugality which was Dutch and a novel (for the Dutch) lack of coziness. The De Stijl group of artist-craftsmen-philosophers, including Theo van Doesburg, Piet Mondrian, and Gerrit Rietveld, had an immense effect on twentieth-century art and the design of many products. They believed in an art which was to seek universality rather than subjective expression, which was to be a guide by which man could control his environment. The members of De Stijl felt a strong attachment to straight lines, right angles, and primary colors. Its principles were purely expressed in Rietveld's architecture and furniture, in which the joints are visible and the separateness of each component is emphasized. Planes are flat, the chairs have no curves to fit the human frame; they are independent objects, constructed with assertive austerity. Though people have been known to claim they are comfortable, it is perhaps because the furniture suits a Calvinist disposition that expects forthrightness rather than softness, discipline rather than compromise. In the new sections of Amsterdam planned by Hendrik Berlage the mood is less severe, and the rather heavy formality of large blocks of flats has in time been alleviated by trees, ivy, and grass, and by variety of use: houses, shops, and small hotels often occupying the same building.

War once more. This time Holland did not manage to preserve her neutrality. On May 10, 1940, Hitler's armies invaded the Low Countries. Holland lasted five days, and in Belgium Leopold and his troops, bottled up near the coast, stuck it out for eighteen days before they capitulated under heavy pressure. The British, however, had been given time to make their heroic evacuation from Dunkirk and took with them part of the Belgian government. Leopold remained a passive prisoner of the Germans in the château of Laeken; those who left to continue the fight from abroad blamed him for giving up. The Luxembourgers did not try to stay neutral, as they had in 1914. They declared war on the Germans in May and were quickly overrun. Their Prince Jean served in a British regiment first as a private, then with a commission. The Dutch were already arranging a surrender on the day the Germans bombed Rotterdam—their planes first destroying the city's water supply, then dropping incendiaries. Nine hundred people were killed, 78,500 were made homeless, and though when compared to some of the German and Allied air raids made later in the war it might seem small-scale, it was the first horrendous taste in the West of a *blitzkrieg*. Queen Wilhelmina, followed by her government's ministers, went into exile in London, where she made periodic broadcasts of encouragement to the Dutch people. (Churchill once praised her as "the greatest man I know.")

Under German occupation the Low Countries suffered mounting hardships as the war went on. The Germans carried off machinery, manufactured goods, raw materials, food, and people. Clothes were irreplaceable; leather shoes vanished altogether. Sickness and malnutrition were prevalent. Children in school fainted from hunger and city families pedaled to visit rural relatives or friends who might have food to spare. Fuel was so scarce that neighbors came round to the one house in a locality that had a fire in the stove. In Amsterdam, during the last winter of the war, empty houses were ripped apart for the firewood they might contain; they were in great part houses of Jews.

Among the many people deported from the Low Countries by the Germans were half a million Belgians. After March, 1942, men between the ages of eighteen and fifty and unmarried women between eighteen and thirty-five were recruited forcibly for labor in Germany. Of the eighty thousand Belgian Jews, some fifteen hundred survived the war. In the case of Holland, Hitler and Himmler toyed with the idea of deporting the entire Dutch nation once they had given up as impracticable the notion of incorporating the Dutch—then presumed to be of good Aryan stock—in the Third Reich. But eventually it was mainly the Jews who were carried away. Some 140,000 of them lived in Holland before the war, 110,000 were deported, and of these all but 5,000 died in the camps and gas chambers. Eight thousand survived in

World War II photographs of (clockwise) Germans invading Holland, the destruction of Rotterdam, American troops in Belgium, and a Belgian air raid

Holland by going into hiding. Some, like the Frank family, hid with the courageous help of Dutch friends, but were caught by the Germans before the war ended. Anne Frank, a thirteen-year-old girl, left a diary which is a vital record of their condition. She noted how Dutch children were begging for bread, and, with superb courage, she expressed her own feelings of good fortune for being in hiding. Although there was no nationwide heroism, there were great acts of courage. The Amsterdam dock workers went on strike to protest against the registration of Jews. University professors resigned, and students refused to attend classes. Many people hid Jews at the cost of their own security and sometimes of their own lives.

Of course, some resisted, some collaborated, and most people as in other occupied countries simply tried to keep alive as safely as they could in a world where they could be shipped off to work in Germany or arrested for listening to the radio—in 1943 the Germans attempted to confiscate all the radio sets in Holland. Broadcasts from London kept the Dutch up to date with progress in the war against the Germans. It was a world of identity cards and the black market, where "real money" lost real value and was often replaced by the exchange of services or the barter of clothes, jewels, and pictures. Dutch fascists took the opportunity to become local bullies, while in Belgium members of an authoritarian Christian movement, the Rexists, and of a Flemish nationalist party, the VNV, collaborated with the Germans. Some Rexists served with the German army on the Russian front. A few Flemings joined SS groups. But they were far outnumbered by those who served with the resistance. Several hundred secret news sheets published information about German looting and named those collaborating with the Germans. Much information about Nazi defenses was sent to London, and many Allied agents and prisoners were helped to escape. A group of *maquis* based in the forested hills of the Ardennes included King Leopold's brother Charles. Sabotage was conducted widely, and— equally important—the Germans were prevented from carrying out a great deal of destruction as they were retreating in the last stages of the war. In Holland many of the two or three hundred thousand who went underground—*fietsers* (cyclists) or *onderduikers* (divers) as they were called—were helped by clandestine organizations. Most of the early members of these underground aid groups were devout Calvinists.

After their first fatalistic feeling that God had sent the Germans to punish them for past wrongdoing, the Calvinists came round to the belief that the Germans were anti-Christ, and thus had to be actively opposed. The resistance aid organizations distributed books to those in hiding, and, when they could, thwarted black market profiteering—in one instance scuttling the fishing boats of men they thought were doing too well from a town's hunger. Those who went underground often led a rabbit-like existence. Holland has no wilderness or outback; men hid in haylofts and rootcellars, cupboards and attics, sometimes for years.

Perhaps the only story of success in that period of Dutch history concerns the painter Jan van Meegeren. Van Meegeren had discovered what he called a Vermeer in 1937; his account was that it had turned up in the possession of an old Dutch family long resident in France. Van Meegeren sold this painting to the Boymans Museum in Rotterdam. During the war Van Meegeren "found" five more Vermeers, one of which he sold to Field Marshall Goering for 1,650,000 guilders. After the war, accused of handing over Dutch national treasures to the enemy, Van Meegeren made the defense that they had not been national treasures—they had not been Vermeers at all. Rather they had been Van Meegerens—all his own work. Nevertheless the forgeries had been so skillful that Van Meegeren had to paint a further Vermeer in prison to prove his case. (And the Boymans Museum seems to remain not altogether convinced about its own Vermeer/Van Meegeren: in recent years its acquisition was installed in semihiding near the director's room but is now hung closer to the public galleries.) Many undisputed masterpieces by Vermeer and Rembrandt survived the war buried in the coastal dunes or the caves of Limburg.

The liberation of Belgium took place in 1944. The British Second Army entered Brussels; Antwerp was freed by British and Canadian forces with the help of the Belgian resistance; and the U.S. First Army moved into southern Belgium to take Liège and Namur. There were joyous celebrations, despite the V-bombs and the German offensive in the Ardennes still to come. However, Field Marshall Montgomery's attempt to precipitate the German retreat from the Netherlands by an airborne attack on Arnhem failed badly, and Holland had to endure another winter under the Germans. It is remembered as "the hunger winter," when the Dutch ate tulip bulbs.

CHAPTER X

PROVINCES
OF THE NEW EUROPE

Events in the postwar period have emphasized some of the differences among the Low Countries. In other respects, however, the times have tended to place both Holland and Belgium within a similar framework, in which they are subjected to similar problems, and similar responses are evoked. First of all, the differences: Belgium recovered more quickly from the Second World War, which was over virtually a year earlier than in Holland. Austerity had to be endured a much shorter time, together with a brief period of unsettled currency and uneasy politics—the latter aggravated by the problems of dealing with collaborators. There was also the problem of handling the return of the king, which dragged on until 1951 and was finally resolved by Leopold's abdication in favor of his son Baudouin. Belgium's recovery from the war (faster than that of any other occupied country) was helped by the fact that the Germans had not removed as much industrial machinery as they had done during the First World War; their rapid withdrawal on this occasion left much less devastation. The food shortage was soon over and factories were working full time. The new all-party coalition government set about improving social legislation,

"The Castle of the Pyrenees" by René Magritte, who attempted, as one critic put it, "to bring into disrepute the whole apparatus of bourgeois reality"

increasing pensions, health insurance, paid holidays, and family allowances. All seemed well. Yet within ten years cracks in this apparently solid edifice had begun to show. After the profitable pleasures of the Brussels World Fair in 1958, the Congo erupted. People began to realize that Belgium had been living beyond its true means for many years. Furthermore, having entered the Industrial Revolution earlier than most countries, Belgium like Britain was now affected by industrial senility—many plants had simply grown too old, and because they had survived the war without damage, had not been replaced or rejuvenated. Many industries now needed great subsidies. The Belgian coal industry, for example, still needed a subsidy of 110 million francs in 1969. Steel was produced in antique mills, a long way from the sea. As the postwar seller's market disappeared, and other countries brought forth competitive goods from new, better located, more efficient factories, Belgium abruptly had its high standard of living put in doubt. The nation went looking for foreign investment.

These postwar industrial problems did not ease the crucial Belgian dilemma of language and regional differences. Walloon provinces were stuck with the most obsolete industry, worn-out coal mines, antiquated steel plants. New industrial expansion concentrated in Flanders on coastal sites handy for transshipment overseas. Chemical and petroleum industries developed around Antwerp. Towns such as Malines offered cheap land and fuel to new industry. Moreover, Flanders and Brabant provided a ready and experienced body of workers who were, some observers felt, less prone to strike than their Walloon colleagues. (The Flemings perhaps had been out of work more frequently, and in the past Flemish agriculture had been seriously depressed.) Certainly Flanders now became the area of growth. Outside the big cities Flemish families averaged four children to a family, while the birthrate in the Walloon provinces was said to be the lowest in the world: roughly one child to a family.

The fact that Flemings have now acquired a majority in Belgium—5.5 million Flemings compared to 3 million Walloons—makes the Walloons, who have ruled the roost too long, more than a little gloomy. The shift of power is reflected in various ways. The Flemings, underrepresented in the Belgian parliament, in 1965 were given more seats in the Lower House. The shifts of population put the language frontier under pressure, and changes have had to be made. Some villages in the east near Fouron have been taken into the Flemish zone amid great protest. On the other hand, Brussels, which is situated in Flemish Brabant, north of the language frontier, is now 80 per cent French-speaking. As it grows and sprawls, it threatens Flemish villages. The new city dwellers, joined by foreign businessmen and people connected with such international organizations as NATO and the Common Market, tend to be non-Flemish-speaking. Since 1963 Flemish-speaking families are supposed to send their children to Flemish schools; but the status-seeking parents have not always wanted to do this. The new dominance of the Flemings (who generally know French) threatens the Walloons (who less often learn Flemish). Religion complicates the matter, for the Catholic Flemings still look on their Walloon compatriots as atheists and freethinkers.

The language problem has naturally bedeviled postwar politics in Belgium. Catholic and socialist parties have each been divided into Walloon and Flemish contingents which run their own separate campaigns. Since 1958 there have been two nationwide systems of schools, Church and secular. At the University of Louvain language problems have been behind student strikes, fights between townspeople and students, and have actually caused governments to fall. Since 1968, the university has been divided and the Walloon section is being moved twelve miles away to Ottignies. In the same year the Ministry of Culture was split into two—there are now two ministers of culture, two education ministers, and two liaison ministers. All of this, needless to say, is exceptionally wasteful of public funds. Setting up (and paying for) two of everything has become a way out of many apparently intractable Belgian domestic problems. On the other hand, one sometimes feels that the Belgians—Flemish and Walloons—get worked up about this old feud because it is old and traditional and they have very little else to get worked up about.

Holland had an immediate postwar period of hard work and austerity. Forty per cent of the country's production capacity had been lost; 92,000 houses had been destroyed; 228,000 acres of land were inundated when the dikes were destroyed, and farms were producing half their prewar crops. Imports exceeded exports by a great margin and had to be paid for by foreign loans and the sale of Dutch overseas invest-

ments. Wages and prices were strictly controlled. In 1948, Holland was on the edge of bankruptcy, precipitated by the huge foreign debt and other factors: lack of raw materials, low productivity, and the postwar loss of Indonesia. The Marshall Plan came as a partial salvation— the United States relieved Holland's balance of payments for the time being, while Holland agreed to produce a balanced budget, a stable currency, and intensified agricultural and industrial efforts. Thus, three years after the war, rationing of milk, sugar, bread, and soap came to an end. In 1948, moreover, the Benelux customs unions (which had been agreed upon in 1944) came into effect. There was no immediate or dramatic impact for Belgium, the Netherlands, and Luxembourg, but a prefiguring of a greater community to come. What doubtless affected most people in the Netherlands during those bleak years was the housing shortage; in some cases young men and women were prevented from getting married, because their home would have to be with parents or parents-in-law; and in other cases they were induced to have children, because houses were allotted to large families.

Modern times, with modern problems and modern answers to some of them, did not make the Netherlands immune to the chance of natural catastrophe. The sea was still there. In January, 1953, a great winter storm coincided with high tide on the Dutch coast. A northwest gale thrust the waters of the North Sea into the funnel beween England and the Low Countries. In the delta region between Rotterdam and Antwerp the sea rose higher than ever before, the waves smashing some dikes and washing over others. Men labored heroically, trying to plug the gaps and raise the dikes with sandbags, but four hundred thousand acres of land were inundated, and nearly two thousand people lost their lives. Farms and livestock were destroyed. It took seven years for Dutch agricultural production to recover from this storm, and since then the Dutch have been making as certain as they can that it never happens again. An impressive system of barrier dams, dikes, bridges, and sluices is being constructed in the delta region, diverting the flow of the Rijn, helping to push back the intruding salt water and to irrigate the Zeeland fields. Another objective has been the shortening of the vulnerable coastline by filling in some of the numerous estuaries. In this process, some things have been lost; small fishing harbors and, in the East Scheldt, oyster and mussel beds. But more important, the chances of

Tranquil tulip gardens in present-day Holland serve as a lingering reminder of the Netherlands' former "tulip madness."

flood disaster in the delta have been reduced to roughly one in ten thousand. The bridges and roadways along the new dams have also had the effect of lessening the isolation of the Zeeland islands.

All in all, although Holland continues to sink and the North Sea goes on rising, the Dutch are keeping ahead of it. Their coastline was 1,230 miles long in 1840; it is roughly 840 miles now. When the delta project is completed in 1980 the coastline will have been shortened to 420 miles. Since the year 1200, some 1,700,000 acres have been gained, 1,400,000 acres lost. For the last half century about 2 per cent of the national income has been spent in dredging, diking, and draining.

After World War II the Low Countries ceased to be colonial powers. Holland lost its empire first. The war brought the Japanese into the Indonesian archipelago, and the Indonesians found what some of them knew already—that their Dutch masters were indispensable. (In 1940 only 221 of 3,092 senior civil servants in the islands were Indonesian.) Premier Sukarno proclaimed the independence of Indonesia on August 17, 1945, and though for three years the Dutch tried forcibly to reinstate themselves, finally they gave it up as a bad job. A Dutch-Indonesian Union, involving an independent Indonesian Republic, lasted until 1954, when this last formal link was severed. The Dutch had to learn how to live without their empire, from which they had got so much. Before the war the Dutch East Indies had supplied some 90 per cent of the world's quinine, 86 per cent of its pepper, 37 per cent of its rubber, 19 per cent of its tea, and 17 per cent of its tin, as well as sugar, coffee, oil, and cigar wrappers. One out of seven Dutchmen gained a direct or indirect income from the Indies. Then, abruptly, it was all over. Between 1945 and 1949 two hundred thousand residents of Indonesia came to Holland. Another hundred thousand came between 1950 and 1964. Many were pure Dutch, some were of mixed blood, and others were pure Indonesian, such as the Christian Amboinese who did not want to stay in the new republic. They made the voyage to austere Holland and the Dutch took them in skillfully and hospitably. Committees welcomed the refugee ships. Temporary accommodations were arranged, clothing for a different climate provided, and help given in finding jobs. Room was found in boarding schools for children who arrived without their parents. Twenty-two homes were established for elderly Indonesians.

This loss, and return, had numerous effects. The fact that they no longer had a captive export market gave the Dutch an additional reason for their successful postwar policy of strict economic management, keeping both wages and prices low and promoting industrial expansion. Furthermore, the loss of empire brought about some changes in the Dutch themselves. They threw off some of their old "regents' mentality"; they got rid of a little of their placid burgher fat. And there were other compensations. Indonesian food enlivened the traditional Dutch cuisine. Indo-Chinese restaurants opened in most towns, while in the cheap food stalls *nasi* balls and *loempia* (a form of egg roll) were sold along with *patates frites,* the Dutchman's staple snack.

The Belgian Congo took longer to boil over, but again the Second World War was a factor making for unrest. During the war the Congolese became aware of the rest of the world. The Belgians in the Congo, cut off from home, decided they enjoyed managing by themselves. The reimposition of tight controls from Brussels after the war annoyed both the Congolese and the whites. Moreover, the Congolese resented the continued power of the Catholic Church, particularly as it was felt in all things educational, and the interference of Belgian domestic problems—for instance, the fact that Flemish was a compulsory subject in Congo secondary schools. In 1957 Ghana became independent from Britain, and soon after De Gaulle announced in nearby Brazzaville that the French colonies could have independence whenever they wanted it. The Mouvement National Congolais, led by Patrice Lumumba, gained increasing support and created more and more unrest. In January, 1959, riots, looting, and killing occurred in Leopoldville, as the army moved in. Belgium reacted in shock, and with unconsidered haste decided to let the Congolese have their independence, for which no real plans had been made. Tribal fighting began. Belgian capital and technicians fled. When Belgian troops went in to protect what remained, Lumumba's new government called for United Nations troops. The province of Katanga, rich in copper and cobalt, proclaimed its independence, with the prompting of Belgian business interests.

Thus the separation between Belgium and her colony was drawn out and bloody. It caused the deaths of Lumumba and, indirectly, of Dag Hammarskjöld of the UN, several bouts of migration in and out by Belgian experts, and the seizure of Belgian assets by the government

of General Joseph Mobutu. The process of decolonization involved the renaming of towns—Leopoldville became Kinshasa—and the Congo is now the nation of Zaire. There were demonstrations against the Belgians in foreign cities like Cairo and Moscow. Missionaries stuck to their missions and mercenaries revolted, while a giant Congolese industrial concern was created to take over from the Belgian industrial giant. The lawyers prospered throughout, working out transfer agreements and compensations. The hatred of the white Belgians was balanced by the Congolese need for their knowledge and capital. The pendulum swung frequently from love to hate and back again, but by the late 1960s the situation had become fairly stable under Mobutu's authoritarian government. Widespread bloodletting has ceased, though occasionally an erstwhile rival politician is assassinated. A treaty of friendship between Belgium and the Congo was signed in 1970. It can perhaps be said that in the history of decolonization, Holland and Belgium did not do very well, but—remembering Nigeria and Algeria—their record was not much worse than other nations'.

In both Low Countries the postwar years have seen the growth of what might be called the concerned state—a complementary growth

Although land reclamation projects and pollution pose serious threats to Dutch fisheries, many Netherlanders still earn their livelihood from the sea.

being that of government, and the number of people working for it. A good deal of forethought and planning has gone into removing friction and risk from daily life. There have been few strikes. Much negotiation goes on between management and workers' representatives all the time. In Belgium industrial wages and most professional wages are linked to the cost of living. Employers have strict obligations to their employees, including three weeks paid holiday every year and long periods of notice before firing. The employers pay about half the cost of the social security scheme, which in Belgium is run by the trade unions and provides unemployment and sickness benefits and old-age pensions. In Holland employers and employees share the contributions to the Sick Fund through which private insurance companies take care of medical expenses—nearly three quarters of the population is covered by it, although those wealthy enough may look after themselves. The Netherlands had a particularly peaceful record in labor relations until the end of the sixties, when the inflation that affected much of the world also caused trouble in Holland. In general, the machinery of compromise has seemed to be well oiled. The sociologist Jacob Goudsblom has written: "The conflicts between labor and management have not disappeared, but both parties have conceded in the acceptance of a set of rules providing for settlement by orderly means. In the Netherlands this development has gone further than in other countries."

The Low Countries are now packed with people. Holland is the most densely populated country in the world, with 13 million people living on roughly 14,000 square miles, and Belgium lies second. Belgium on nearly 12,000 square miles has 9.6 million people. Luxembourg's population of 340,000 has proportionately more space in its 999 square miles. In Holland the pressure of population has considerably affected what has been done with the environment. Even in the seventeenth century Holland was highly urbanized. Today the belt of old towns—Dordrecht, Rotterdam, Delft, The Hague, Leiden, Haarlem, Zaandam, Amsterdam, and Utrecht—forms an urban horseshoe: the Randstad, or Rim-City, as the Dutch call it. Within this conurbation live nearly 4.5 million people. In other words, some 40 per cent of the Dutch live on 5 per cent of the land area of the Netherlands.

Tight fit has bred an instinct for planning. Men whose ancestors labored together on the dikes to keep out the sea respect a communal

endeavor to make sure the whole country is not overwhelmed by a sea
of people. Dutch cities do not sprawl. The soggy nature of the land
makes it impossible to build just anywhere. Construction sites have to
be carefully prepared at great expense with drainage, land fill, and pil-
ings for foundations. This preparation is now largely conducted by the
municipalities, which also own most of their own land, and this helps
in the preservation of strict controls on land use, and consequent sharp
breaks between town and country—and indeed, in preserving wedges
of country between the towns. Despite the urgent postwar demand for
housing, the Randstad has a large green core due in part to good planning, in part to the presence in considerable numbers of greenhouse
farmers and bulbgrowers with land demands of their own.

Life is not particularly easy with such a space shortage. The Dutch
have had to get used to elbow-to-elbow living conditions, dwelling in
small apartments, looking at pictures in packed museums, and shopping in perilously crowded streets where trams, bikes, cars, trucks, and
pedestrians struggle for room. Space for recreation is in short supply,
and the lakes, woods, and dunes have to be carefully husbanded. Drinking water is hard to come by, and the Rhine, which flows down with
water from industrial Germany and France, is so tainted with chemicals
and waste by the time it reaches Rotterdam that complicated purification processes make the water barely drinkable. Around Rotterdam,
moreover, the air becomes thick with fumes from refineries and petro-
chemical plants. A network of pollution-sensing devices is being established so that when conditions become dangerous production can be
temporarily halted.

Yet many of the Randstad towns reflect the charm and character they
have acquired over the centuries. Narrow streets and canals running
through them, lined with brick houses, preserve the scale of a less con-
gested time. Despite contemporary demands for offices, apartments,
and a new metropolitan subway system, the center of Amsterdam retains the basic form established in the seventeenth century. Amsterdam-
ers still cherish the 1611 expansion plan which laid out the four
semicircular canals: Herrengracht, Keizersgracht, Prinsengracht, and
the Singel. There are still in all a hundred canals in Amsterdam, a
hundred thousand trees (many replanted to replace those burned for
firewood during the Second World War), and five thousand buildings

from the seventeenth and eighteenth centuries. Dutch planners and architects do not generally seem to regard this inheritance as a constraint or millstone around their necks, but rather as an exemplary challenge.

Sir William Temple noted in the seventeenth century the Dutch willingness to be taxed for public projects. "This makes the beauty and strength of their towns, the commodiousness of travelling in their country . . . the pleasantness of their walks . . . and, in short, the beauty, convenience, and sometimes magnificence, of all public works, to which every man pays as willingly, and takes as much pleasure and vanity in them, as those of other countries do in the same circumstances, among the possessions of their families, or private inheritance." The Dutch now invest in planning for the year 2000, with the knowledge that given such shortage of space, organization of their resources is the only answer. They pay for the creation of a human landscape, preserving the semiwilderness of the coastal dunes and the wildfowl that flourish on the meers and polders. They attempt to keep at bay the dehumanization that seems to be a corollary of industrial civilization, holding on to the attitudes that produced the *hofjes,* the courtyards of little houses where old people could live, cared for, yet retaining essential independence. Modern *hofjes* exist in apartment blocks or terraces of small houses amid the new developments.

Belgium maintains a far weaker tradition of respect for the commonweal. A visitor passing from one Low Country to the other, from north to south, thinks immediately, "Belgium is messier." Along the Belgian coast there now seems to be a continuous jerry-built town, a ribbon of ramshackle possessiveness, that reminds one of the New Jersey shore or the Sussex coast near Peacehaven. Main roads are frequently still paved with bumpy cobblestones, and drivers have none of the patience and self-discipline that generally characterize the Dutch motorist. (Driving licenses are only a recent innovation in Belgium.) Tax evasion is said to be widespread, as in France.

Despite this, the Belgians have things in common with their northern neighbors. Although the street scene is less tidy, the Belgian housewife is almost as maniacal as her Dutch sister in cleaning, sweeping, dusting, and beating rugs. Belgians, like the Dutch, have a passion for belonging to associations in which they find identity and deep satisfaction. Belgian socialists, having been born in socialist hospitals and educated in socialist schools, join socialist soccer clubs. The comic example that Dutch behavioralists use when discussing the Dutch need for separate groups is the Roman Catholic Goat Breeders Association. Having lived with firm religious and political opinions for so long, the Belgians and Dutch have formed all sorts of societies which allow them to avoid contact with people who hold different ideas and beliefs. The Dutch have rival newspapers, denominational broadcasting services, and separate first aid societies, so that sometimes it seems that all they share in common with each other are roads, utilities, light, and air.

More than in other northern European countries, religion remains a serious concern in both Belgium and Holland. Most Belgians, whether Flemings or Walloons, are Catholic—some 85 per cent; and of that number, more than half are practicing Catholics. As in Ireland, the Church has been heavily involved in politics and trade union affairs. A priest, Guido Gezelle, founded the Flemish national movement in the nineteenth century. Cardinal Van Roey, archbishop of Malines (d. 1961), was a fervent monarchist and fierce opponent of strikers. However, the present archbishop of Malines-Brussels has earned quite a different reputation. At the Second Vatican Council in 1964 Leo Joseph Cardinal Suenens clearly stood for progress and reform in the Church, and since the Council he has spoken out for changes in the Curia and the election of popes.

The Dutch, as they have always done, take religion, or lack of religion, with little lightness. There are still small country towns where the Calvinist dominie condemns Sunday bicycle riding or denounces young couples for buying television sets. But the most conservative Calvinists now make up less than 10 per cent of the population. Another 28 per cent are Protestants of a less strict persuasion—though they may go to church twice on Sundays. Some 40 per cent of the Dutch are Catholics and it is to them that the Dutch reputation for theological controversy has passed. This change has come about rapidly. As recently as 1954 Dutch Catholic bishops forbade their flocks to have any socialist ties, to read socialist newspapers, or join socialist trade unions, on pain of being excluded from the sacraments. Mixed marriages were abhorred. The French author Bernard Pingaud noted that in Holland "to be a Catholic does not merely mean going to Mass on Sundays and regularly to Confession . . . it means buying one's milk from a Catholic milkman, voting for the Catholic party, sending ones' children to a Catholic school, employing only Catholic servants or workmen and having only Catholic friends." But as the Netherlands has become ever more urban, and the time it takes to get from the country into cities shrinks, the Dutch Church seems to reflect the social awareness of the Randstad. At Vatican II, Cardinal Alfrink of Holland interrupted the conservative Italian Cardinal Ottaviani when the latter exceeded the time limit for speeches. Dutch bishops have annoyed Rome by declaring that birth control is a matter for the individual conscience of their parishioners. Catholic discussion groups have speculated with refreshing candor about such dogmas as original sin and virgin birth. Ecumenical meetings and communion feasts with Protestants have been held. Although the number of priests in Holland is falling rapidly, as in many other countries, and clerical celibacy (which the papacy upholds) is under heavy attack, attendance at Mass is higher than in most other nominally Catholic countries. And just as in the nineteenth century three thousand Dutchmen volunteered for the papal army to defend Pio Nono against Garibaldi, so today more than five thousand Dutch priests work as Catholic missionaries in various foreign lands. The Dutch, and Belgian Catholics like Cardinal Suenens, believe they are not being schismatic. They want to change the Church from within and make it more relevant to local and individual experience. This excites them; there is a heady sense that the Low Countries are once again in a position to throw some light on matters that have too long been shelved. In one area, at least, they know they are objects of world curiosity, as they have not been since the seventeenth century.

The times are calling forth loyalties beyond those owed to the nation-state. The Benelux union came into force in 1948 but has since been overshadowed by the European Economic Community, or Common Market. EEC headquarters is in Brussels, as is the headquarters of NATO, which moved there after General De Gaulle in 1967 asked the organization to quit their Paris headquarters. Holland, Belgium, and Luxembourg, feeling that neutrality is no longer a sensible policy for them, are members of NATO. The FN automatic rifle, standard issue for NATO forces, is made in Liège. Paul Henri Spaak, who has often been Belgium's foreign minister, has also been first president of

OVERLEAF: *Youthful unrest in the Low Countries, as elsewhere, is vociferously expressed at demonstrations, like this one led by Dutch students.*

the UN General Assembly, first chairman of the Consultative Assembly of the Council of Europe, and secretary-general of NATO—a post presently held by Dr. Joseph Luns, a frequent foreign minister in Netherlands governments. Belgians and Dutch alike have seen NATO's role as more than just anti-Russian or defensive. In 1966 Pierre Harmel, then Belgian foreign minister, suggested various ways in which NATO could meet the Warsaw Pact members in reciprocal troop reductions, and foster political cooperation among its members.

The entire Low Countries are particularly conscious of being European. It is an awareness which begins to minimize the difference between Belgians and Hollanders—though the differences between Flemings and Walloons or Calvinists and Catholics have not yet lost all substance. Within the Common Market labor is relatively free to cross old national boundaries; passport inspections are often cursory. Antwerp and Rotterdam are increasingly parts of a single vast industrial and transportation complex (Rotterdam is now the largest port in the world). Natural gas from the Dutch North Sea fields is piped to other countries and has gone a long way to replace the lost wealth of the Indies. The Low Countries have a worker shortage and import labor from Greece, Turkey, Morocco, and Spain—so, more than three hundred years after they were expelled, the Spanish are invited back. Europe closes itself firmly around its member countries in many forms. Eurovision shows British soccer teams or French singers to Belgians and Dutchmen alike. Supermarkets sell Spanish wine and Bulgarian canned fruit (though due to the anomalies of agricultural policy, it may still be worthwhile to smuggle Dutch butter into Belgium). Before Britain was admitted to the EEC, her ties with Belgian industry were strong, and two of the largest firms in the world, Shell and Unilever, have twin headquarters in Britain and Holland. And Brussels seems to be staking claim to being the working capital of the new Europe.

In 1969 the executive commission of the Common Market moved (from the well-named Avenue de la Joyeuse Entrée) to the giant Berlaimont Building. The EEC shares this structure with EURATOM (the European Atomic Energy Organization), for which there had earlier been great hopes not only in terms of cheap power but in terms of a practical exchange of ideas; but so far industrial rivalry and nationalist secrecy have dominated the nuclear scene. Indeed, with all its apparatus of community, and all its resident Eurocrats, Brussels as a city expresses rather all the large-scale commercial rapacity of the modern age. It has, of course, always been a great banking town and center of the vast trusts and holding companies that control much of Belgian industry. The Brussels-based Société Générale, the conglomerate set up in 1822 by King William, controls 40 per cent of Belgian iron and steel production, much of the electricity, coal, and nonferrous metal production, and half of all bank deposits and insurance. The manner in which big money gets its way in Brussels is flamboyantly evident in the shoddy office buildings and apartment houses run up by property speculators to take advantage of the current demand.

This demand springs not only from the influx of European civil servants and officials—the Eurocrats—but from all their camp followers. In the wake of "Europe" come large firms and their executives. Their *lingua franca* is English, and they establish their own schools for their children. Around Brussels (as also around The Hague), European and American executive ghettos appear to be forming, successors to the communities formed in previous centuries by Hanseatic merchants in Bruges, the Sephardic Jews in Amsterdam, the pilgrims in Leiden, and the Huguenots in Utrecht.

Many of the discussions in 1971 regarding the accession of Britain to the Common Market took place in Luxembourg. The secretariat of the European parliament (which meets monthly in Strasbourg) has skyscraper headquarters in Luxembourg. The grand duchy, sixty miles long and forty wide, has suffered and enjoyed most of the misfortunes and blessings of the Low Countries in the last hundred years. Following the declaration of its independence and neutrality in 1867, it was occupied by the Germans in both wars. Its 340,000 people, however, have enjoyed somewhat steadier government than Belgium and Holland, with none of the turmoil of party political maneuvering that goes on in the rest of the Low Countries. One man, Pierre Werner, has been prime minister since 1959. The present Grand Duke Jean succeeded his mother Charlotte on her abdication in 1964. The Dutch and the Belgians joke about their tiny sister state—there is the tale, for example, about the tourist who sneezed and passed through Luxembourg without noticing. But Luxembourg can claim with some pride that only twenty people are unemployed in a working population of 145,000. It has a successful steel industry and a popular radio station, based in the old fortress of Luxembourgtown, which is listened to by teenagers all over northern Europe. Despite all the elements of economic unity between Belgium and Luxembourg, a few differences remain. Distilled spirits are highly taxed in Belgium, and many Belgians find it worthwhile to make the short trip to the grand duchy for their *eau de vie*.

Holland by no means lacks the materialistic aspects of society that seem so prevalent in Belgium. The Stock Exchange, designed by Berlage, dominates the Damrak in Amsterdam. The new Netherlands Bank offices rise in an unprepossessing high-rise block over the gardens of the Fredericksplein. But materialism in Holland has also the connotation that everything has value, nothing is wasted. And in recent years, Holland has also produced valuable radical movements. Between 1965 and 1967 the Provos—a youthful movement with anarchist, utopian ambitions—shook the complacency of the prosperous Dutch, provoking, by demonstrations and often humorous self-advertisement, a sense that there was great need for social and political change. The Provos particularly wanted to improve life in Amsterdam: to close the center of the old city to traffic; provide public bicycles, painted white, for free use; reduce air pollution by strict enforcement of regulations and fines; allow homeless families to live temporarily in condemned buildings; and return old center-city houses, now offices, to their former use as homes. The Provos won a seat on the City Council before success and the humdrum nature of much political routine began to pall. Its members can be seen as up-to-date followers of a Low Countries tradition that has included the Mennonites and the Brethren of the Common Life, a tradition which goes on. The Provos have been followed by the Kaboutijers, or Gnomes, some of whose City Council representatives were arrested in September, 1970, for smoking marijuana at a Council session, and by the Dolle Minas, young women whose liberated behavior has demonstrated that there is not much left of the stereotyped Dutch girl who wore starched bonnets and wooden shoes. Although the police have now and then cracked down on the summer hordes of students from all countries sleeping in the Dam, the central square in Amsterdam, the city retains its reputation for great tolerance. It is a place where the thoughtful and the bizarre seem equally welcome. It has the possibility still of tulip madness.

The vitality of contemporary Dutch art is evident in many forms—in the ballet of the Netherlands Dance Theater, in sculpture, in the documentary films of Bert Haanstra and Joris Ivens, in the novels of Willem-Frederik Hermans and the plays of the Flemish writer Hugo Claus. Low Countries history has been illuminated in the last fifty years by Henri Pirenne, Johan Huizinga, and Pieter Geyl, to name a few, and science by the physicist Hendrik Lorentz, Pieter Zeeman, Jacobus van't Hoff, and Peter Debye. Two notable modern architects in Holland are Aldo van Eyck and Herman Hertzberger.

At this point the Low Countries have had long experience in the role of being small nations; they have also—looking further into the past —served their time as portions of larger groupings, the Frankish kingdom and the Hapsburg empire. Now as the world shrinks and new federations of states or associations like the Common Market appear, the Low Countries may be helpful harbingers of the future. In their smallness they demonstrate the advantages of human scale and locality. As Friesland retains its identity within the Netherlands, and as the Flemings and Walloons go on bickering within Belgium, so local idiosyncracies may survive within the framework of Europe. Within a European context the Fleming-Walloon feud will seem perhaps less serious particularly as both Flemings and Walloons learn English. Some of the larger and more dangerous animosities that in the past have caused armies to invade the region can scarcely hold in a time when so many crucial problems overlap, when German and French pollution affects the coffee drunk in Rotterdam, and the holiday closing of Ruhr factories (uncoordinated with Dutch vacations) overcrowds the Dutch coastal hotels and beaches. The Low Countries are thus losing their "minor" status in exchange for a significant place in a greater world. With their states as provinces of the new Europe, the Dutch and Belgians may choose to call themselves Netherlanders or Europeans, or once again, as in the Middle Ages, refer simply to themselves as citizens of a specific place—city, town, or village. Already Pieter Geyl's admonition proves unnecessary: "I preach no hostility to the modern state. . . . But I do warn the historian, and the national historian, not to surrender his mind to it unquestioningly."

CHRONOLOGY

3000–1000 B.C.	Early peoples build *terpen* (mounds) as refuges above sea level
c. 57	Caesar conquers the Belgae in northwestern Gaul
15	Incorporation of the Low Countries into the Roman province of Gallia Belgica; spread of Roman culture
A.D. 69–70	Julius Civilis leads abortive Batavian revolt against Romans
c. 200–c. 300	North Sea washes over northern marshes and forms Zuider Zee
c. 400	Roman occupation ends with withdrawal of last Roman legions
c. 500–c. 700	Frankish kings impose authority over Low Countries; Christianity spreads in southern regions, but paganism still thrives
768–814	Charlemagne inaugurates an era of peace in Low Countries
843	By Treaty of Verdun much of Low Countries goes to Lothair
c. 800–c. 1000	Viking invasions ravage Low Countries
c. 900–c. 1300	Rise of small, autonomous principalities governed by local counts who owe allegiance to rulers of France, England, or Germany; growth of towns and textile industry
c. 1250–1400	Era of urban insurrections and peasant uprisings
1302	The Matins of Bruges: Flemish workers massacre French overlords
1356	Joyous Entry of Brabant, early charter of liberties
1384	William Beukels of Zeeland invents salted herring
1384–1447	Dukes of Burgundy bring Low Countries (including duchy of Luxembourg) under one rule
1466?–1536	Desiderius Erasmus, Dutch theologian, scholar, and humanist
1477	Charles the Bold in battle against Swiss at Nancy; the Low Countries pass to Austrian Hapsburgs and France
1519–1555	Charles V, Holy Roman Emperor, rules the Netherlands
1520	Lutheranism begins to take hold in Low Countries; Charles V institutes Inquisition to discourage Protestantism
1548	Charles V organizes the Low Countries into the "Seventeen Provinces" of the Netherlands
1555–1598	Philip II of Spain inherits Low Countries from his father, Charles V, and continues policy of religious persecution
1567	Philip II sends duke of Alba to Netherlands to suppress Protestantism and uprisings of aristocracy against Spanish rule
1568–1648	The Eighty Years' War: the Netherlands fights for independence from Spain under leadership of William the Silent
c. 1550–c. 1570	Calvinism begins to spread in Low Countries
1576	Pacification of Ghent: treaty by which provinces of the Low Countries agree to unite to fight against Spain
1579	Union of Utrecht: southern provinces (roughly Belgium and Luxembourg) make separate peace with Spain
1579–1581	Northern provinces declare their independence and form United Provinces of the Netherlands
c. 1600–c. 1675	Golden Age of the Netherlands; exploration, trade, art, and science flourish; growth of Amsterdam and colonial empire

1602	Dutch East India Company formed
1648	Peace of Westphalia: the Republic of the United Provinces is recognized; Spanish Hapsburgs retain southern provinces
1689	Stadholder William III of Orange becomes king of England
1700–1800	Decline of Dutch political leadership and naval power
1701–1714	War of the Spanish Succession: the Dutch suffer losses, and Spanish Netherlands goes to the Austrian Hapsburgs
1780–1790	Austrian Hapsburg emperor Joseph II imposes reforms on Belgians: in 1789 they form short-lived republic
1792	Belgium is invaded by French Revolutionary armies
1795–1806	United Provinces become Batavian Republic, a French satellite
1797	Belgium is ceded to France by Treaty of Campo Formio
1806–1810	Napoleon abolishes Batavian Republic and creates the kingdom of Holland, with his brother Joseph Bonaparte as monarch
1813	The former kingdom of Holland regains independence from France
1814–1815	Napoleon is defeated at Waterloo in Belgium; the Congress of Vienna recognizes the kingdom of the Netherlands (comprising Holland and Belgium) under William I, Prince of Orange; Luxembourg is incorporated as a grand duchy into the German Confederation and given to William I as his personal property
1830	Belgians declare independence from kingdom of Netherlands
1831	Leopold I, of Saxe-Coburg-Gotha, becomes king of Belgium
1839	Holland recognizes Belgium's sovereignty; French-speaking Luxembourg goes to Belgium; German-speaking, to William I
1867	Luxembourg is declared an independent, neutral state; it remains in personal union with Netherlands
1876–1885	Leopold II of Belgium forms the Congo Free State in Africa
1890	Luxembourg passes to Adolph of Nassau after death of William III
1908	Congo Free State is ceded to Belgium: it becomes Belgian Congo
1914–1918	World War I: Germany invades Belgium, occupies Luxembourg; Holland remains neutral
1918	Holland initiates plan for enclosure and reclamation of Zuider Zee
1928	Completion of dike creating fresh-water Lake IJssel
1940–1945	World War II: Leopold III of Belgium surrenders to Germany; rulers of Netherlands and Luxembourg go into exile in England
1947	Benelux economic union is formed
1949	All Low Countries join NATO; the Netherlands recognizes independence of Indonesia
1958	The Low Countries join EEC (Common Market) and EURATOM
1960	Belgium grants independence to Belgian Congo
1970	City of Luxembourg elects first woman mayor, Colette Flesch

CREDITS AND INDEX

The author is indebted to the writings of the following: S. J. de Laet, Marc Bloch, Christopher Dawson, Henri Pirenne, Johan Huizinga, Pieter Geyl, B. H. M. Vlekke, R. H. Tawney, Norman Cohn, John J. Murray, Paul Zumthor, J. L. Motley, A. J. Barnouw, A. de Meeüs, Charles Wilson, Margot Lyon, B. Pingaud, Eugene Fromentin, Bruce Grant, Johan Goudsblom, W. Warmbrunn, Jacob Presser, and Anthony Sampson; and also to the observations of Tacitus, Caesar, Boswell, and Sir William Temple.

Page numbers in **boldface type** refer to illustrations.
Page references to map entries are in *italic type.*